My Life With a Sociopath

It Can Happen To Anyone…

Karen Ferguson

Copyright

 This edition published: May 2022 by Chronos Publishing

ISBN: 978-1-914529-34-4 Paperback
ISBN: 978-1-914529-35-1 E-book

This book is part autobiographical, reflecting the author's present recollections of experiences over time.

Some names and identifying details have been changed to protect the privacy of individuals.

Cover Design by Danje Designs

Acknowledgements

With heartfelt thanks to:-

My Dad, the best man I know, who not only gave a home to me and my children, but who kept me going throughout all of this.

And to my children, because I love them.

Contents

Prologue

He drove his car into my house today.

He told me he was going to do it, I didn't believe him, but he did, he drove straight through my kitchen wall, missing my niece by about two inches.

It was of course the final straw, the one that broke the camel's back, well broke any hope I had of this ending in a rational way.

If you asked me even last year, could I put into words what had happened I'd have categorically said, 'no'! It's only now that I can look back and start to assess the way in which my life was slowly controlled and eroded.

I never thought that I would be writing this story, telling the world what happened to me, but it did happen and so I am. Like all stories, of course we have to start at the beginning.

Introduction

I decided to use many of the text message conversations, rather than just writing a narrative, because I felt that it was important to show the reality of my experience. If I just wrote the 'story' it would probably seem unrealistic and made up and wouldn't convey the persistence of his messages, or the way he jumped from nice to nasty in an instant. I am not sure that I could do justice for want of a better word, to what really happened, if I had glossed over the nitty gritty of life with someone who is abusive. It made sense to me to show it how it was, to show how the slow erosion effect took over and changed me and how the constant switching of his personality left me both unable to always gauge situations correctly and afraid to say certain things.

After guiding you through some of our history, you will find yourself reading the actual messages and some of the conversations that passed between us, him on the left and me on the right. I haven't included all of the messages because some of them are just day to day comments and therefore not really relative. The reason I have included some but not all of our actual conversations, haven't included many of the actual conversations, a lot of which were very abusive, is simply because my memory of them is not clear enough to be able to offer them accurately.

I can't give you chapter and verse of our whole relationship, not just because so much happened, but because I have blocked some of it out, or as they say in therapy terms, I normalised it to the point that maybe I felt that that was just how my life was.

What I am going to do, is to share with you some of these experiences, the good, the bad and the downright ugly.

It wasn't all bad, at least not the first few years, I am sure it wasn't, the good must have outweighed the bad, and I did love him.

I am aware that in some places I may come across as cold, unfeeling or even ungrateful, and I can understand why people might interpret my comments like this. Looking back I know that I did learn to become a different person, not because it is who I am, but because it was the way I learnt to cope with what was happening. It was easier to become harder, at least on the outside, as it was preferable to feeling weak.

So if you read, or perhaps it might be better to say, see these elements of me in this book, understand that I am none of these things, I simply developed a mechanism to cope.

I'm really quite petrified of this book being published, because I know I am potentially opening myself up to being judged or criticised, but I have faced worse and I will not let these things stop me. It is a story that needs to be told and if it helps just one person, then it will have been worth it.

Chapter 1
The Beginning

I loved him, I honestly believe that I did, so much so, that I couldn't imagine my life without him. More importantly to the story, I trusted him, he was my comfort when things were tough and when he told me during these times that everything would be ok, I believed him. I thought I was safe, that he loved me, that he cared about me and that we would be together for the rest of our lives.

I got a job as a Resort Manager working in Spain. It was in a relatively small place in the Costa Brava called L'Estartit. I'd never worked abroad before and despite a few hiccups, it was probably the best job I had ever had.

He worked part time for another one of the holiday companies based on the same site and we met a few weeks into the season. He used to tell me that he had tried talking to me several times but that I hadn't paid him any attention. Whilst I am not disputing his version, I think I was just so busy having fun and working hard, that in all honesty, I don't think I even noticed him to begin with.

If I remember correctly, the first time I actually remember noticing him, he was on stage dressed as an alien, the creation of one of the kid's clubs and he had a toilet brush on his head.

Maybe I noticed him then because he seemed to be confident enough to be on stage and secure enough to be able to make a fool of and laugh at himself.

A week or so later, I was out with some of my friends, either at a local bar, or maybe it was at the onsite disco, I can't remember, but he bought me a drink, we talked for hours, he made me laugh and I felt safe with him.

I don't mean that I generally didn't feel safe, but he was well built, he smiled a lot, seemed very confident and it was easy to be in his company.

I hadn't gone to Spain to find a partner, but I had been single for a while and I guess, at least in part, I was very flattered that this confident man was clearly so interested in me. Don't get me wrong, it wasn't one sided, I did genuinely enjoy his company.

We spent a great deal of time together and he asked me to marry him just two weeks after our first date. Mad I know, but I was so sure, I was absolutely certain that this was the man I was going to marry. I had been offered a job for the winter and then the same management job back for the next summer. I really loved my job and I was fully intending to return the next year, even though I ended up turning down the winter job as we were planning to get married during that time.

Although I had a job to return to, he didn't, but it seemed that he had a good reputation and had been working abroad for years, so neither of us doubted he would be able to find something and return with me the following year.

We came back to the UK at the end of the season, we booked our wedding and a few months later I found out that I was pregnant, everything just seemed to fall into place, I was happy and he certainly seemed to be as well.

I was disappointed that I couldn't go back to Spain, so much so, that I even contacted the company I had worked for to see if it was possible. Unfortunately, due to the approximate date my son was due, part way through the busiest part of the season, it just wasn't possible.

We moved in with my parents, with talks about moving to France and starting our lives together there, we even visited a couple of times to look at property. He owned a flat, had a small income from shares in a family company and a car, and he assured me that money wasn't an issue, I believed him, I had no reason not to.

Then when I was about five months pregnant with my son, I found out that the CSA were chasing him for money for a child that had been born when he was about eighteen. He swore it wasn't his, that the only reason his name was on the birth certificate was because the child's mother had told him he was the father and at the time he believed her.

It was a really big shock, after all, he had led me to believe that our child was his first but I guess we all have a history and although I wasn't happy, we were getting married and I trusted what he told me.

Even then, life was rather up and down if I'm honest but he had found a job, not a great one, but he was working and bringing in an income and that was the important thing.

He promised me it would all be alright and I wanted to believe him, so I did, and life carried on. We moved into our first home, he got a job as a bus driver and although he worked shifts, he seemed to enjoy it.

A couple of months later and our son was born. He was good with Jack, he never minded feeding or changing him, took his turns putting him to bed, getting up during the night and gave me time to rest when I needed it.

But, as with every Dr Jekckyl, there needs to be a Mr. Hyde.

He would fly off the handle now and then, I couldn't tell you what triggered it, he would suddenly announce he wasn't going to do something that was planned and often took money from my purse, but he always had a reason and I loved him, so I just let it go.

The thing is, I wasn't naive, I knew deep down it wasn't right, that the relationship wasn't as I had hoped but life has a way of keeping you in there, it's easier to stay and hope it improves, believe the lies and the half truths rather than start again alone.

Time moved forward, life seemed to carry on but as much as I would like to say otherwise, the financial issues just seemed to get worse as time went on.

I loved my son, he was the brightness during the dark days. We never really did much, because I didn't have money for treats, but we were always together and we played a lot. He was a bright and funny boy, with the cutest smile and a happy disposition. He walked early, talked early and I loved being with him.

Looking back, I guess when Jack started to speak, to push boundaries, as I assume all children do, that that's when he started to change. He would tell Jack off if he looked at him 'funny', or if he fidgeted too much. If we went out he would often threaten to leave where we were or to take Jack home if he didn't stop.

These were the warning signs. Jack was my world and he was always going to come first, so right from the beginning I learnt how to stand up for him, he was my son and I wasn't letting him get hurt. Maybe I was too soft on him, but I didn't care, he was my baby and I was going to protect him.

Don't get me wrong, he never laid a hand on Jack, not until later anyway, but I would often feel sick at the idea of going out, just in case he kicked off.

I should have seen it coming, the signs were there right from the start, but initially love blinded me, then fear and finally I became numb.

Chapter 2
Money

I have written this as a separate chapter because it's the one constant, throughout our time together that caused the majority of our problems. There isn't a single aspect of our lives that wasn't affected by money and he used that aspect to wear me down.

I used to be a very generous person. If I had money, I was more than happy to spend it, I would buy little gifts for my parents, just because I thought they would like them. I earned my own money, I always had enough, and I never borrowed money, so I never owed anything.

But living with him changed me, so drastically, that I am traumatised by the idea of not having enough money and even the thought of being in debt.

I still sometimes panic when I have to spend money, even on food shopping, because I am so afraid of the consequences of not having enough. Actually, I don't even know what 'enough' would be to enable me to feel safe.

Looking back, almost from the beginning there were warning signs. When we were coming back from Spain, he didn't have enough money to pay for his flight, and although I had a great time whilst I was there, I had still saved a portion of my wages, so I paid for his flight.

I didn't really think much of it, he had a flat, a car and an income, so when we got home everything would be sorted out. At least that's what he told me. That was the first of the lies about money, the first time I took him at his word. He even showed me photos of his flat, so why would I have had any reason to doubt him?

A few weeks after we got back to the UK, and with the promise of money from the sale of his flat, I took out a loan for a car and put most of our wedding on a credit card he persuaded me to take out. Again, he told me that once he sold his flat that he would pay off the credit card and I had no reason to not trust him.

I realised sometime later that I should never have let him persuade me, that I should have insisted that we waited until we could afford it. I should have said no, I should have been more assertive and I accept responsibility for that. I was caught up in the wedding, being pregnant, looking to our future and feeling loved that I just didn't see, or perhaps, didn't want to see that maybe I was either making a mistake, or allowing myself to be taken advantage of. You don't meet someone, fall in love with them, and expect them to take advantage of you, do you? It honestly never occurred to me that that was what was happening.

Prior to the wedding I met one of his sister's. She was so lovely, so kind and welcoming, that it probably made me love him a bit more, the fact that she welcomed me so willingly into their family.

I can't remember if it was before our wedding or very soon after, that I found out that he had sold his flat years before, that his shares had been signed over to his sister, much to his disgust and that he didn't even own a car.

He wasn't forthcoming with this information and it was only after I began to question when the flat would be sold, that he gradually admitted everything to me.

He told me that his sister had had to bail him out of the debts he had run up after his first marriage broke down. He was really quite angry that they hadn't helped him more, at least hadn't helped him how he wanted.

Maybe I should have ended it then, but I was pregnant and felt sorry for him. He told me that he had found his first wife in bed with his best friend and he went off the rails and got into debt. I wonder now what story he will concoct to blame me for his debt problems.

No more than six months after we arrived back in the UK, we were already in major debt. The car was soon repossessed, my parents had to bail us out and I was mortified that this had all happened.

Why didn't I just take over dealing with all the finances? Honestly I don't know. It might seem dim but he was a grown adult, and I honestly thought that as he now had a job and was going to be a dad, that things would improve.

Naive I know, well I know now, but at the time I was pregnant, tired, missing Spain and trapped, but he reassured me again and again that everything would be fine and I wanted to believe him. It honestly never occurred to me that someone would lie to this extent. He was so good at convincing me that it would all be alright.

Over the years our money situation got worse and worse, with only short periods of respite.

I can't remember the first time a debt collector turned up at our new home, or when the number of 'red' letters started to arrive. I do remember feeling quite terrified that I couldn't pay any more than the minimum on the credit card each month. The interest just kept piling up, so we went over our limit and it just spiraled out of control.

He talked me into getting a consolidation loan, which I agreed to, I was so worried and thought this would be an opportunity to get back on track, but all that ended up happening was more debt over a longer period of time.

I remember crying because I had never been in this position before, never owed this amount of money and we had no means of paying it back. I tried to get a job, but I really struggled, especially with a young child.

We had a joint bank account by this time, something he talked me into and honestly, it did seem easier having just the one account, especially when it was just him working.

I got a job when Jack was about three. It wasn't a huge income, but it was more than we had been getting and it really did help. The problem was, he just kept spending, not just his wages, but mine as well and we often didn't have enough to cover the bills.

As my income started to go up and because I was self-employed, I got a separate bank account, not just to make it easier for paying taxes, but so that he couldn't touch my money unless I transferred it into our joint account, which I did, often, just to stop him going on and on. He could be relentless. You know how a small child seems to have the endless capacity to grind you down when they constantly ask for something? That was him. He would go on and on until eventually it was easier to give in than to listen to him whine.

Eventually I had enough, and I got another bank account. I paid my share of the bills from my account and he took care of, well was meant to take care of his share from the other account.

That account had an overdraft on it, something he never paid off and eventually, after years and years of charges, the bank said that they didn't like the way the account was being managed and told us they were closing the account. They demanded the overdraft be settled.

I had made the mistake of not taking my name off the account, some of the bills were in my name and they were paid from that account, so I was held accountable for the money as well.

Obviously he didn't have the money, so I had to get a loan pay it off so that the debt was cleared. He wasn't troubled and let's face it, this was one less problem that he had to ignore.

As my work increased, I learnt not to tell him exactly what I was earning, because if he knew I had money, he would push and try to convince me to spend it.

It went against my nature to not share and sometimes I slipped up, if I mentioned that I had some money saved, then he would start. We needed (he wanted) a new car, a holiday, to buy 'stuff'. It didn't really seem to matter what we bought, he just wanted to spend money.

He certainly wasn't tight with money, at least that was the impression he gave. He was the first to offer to pay for drinks when we were out. I think he liked the idea that people thought he had money and that he was generous. Only sometimes, well more than sometimes, I had to give him the money in the first place. You'd never know that he was actually a kept man at this point in our relationship, yes he worked but rarely did he contribute.

He always went over the top at Christmas, spending money on so many inconsequential items, things that were just unnecessary. I never objected to my children having things and if he wanted to spoil them, then I was okay with that.

I bought them things as well, but things they had asked for, and not just 'stuff'. Actually, as they got older, especially my son, would open presents, look at me and ask why he had bought him these things. They were pointless, rubbish gifts that showed how little he knew any of us and that he just liked spending for the sake of spending, buying things was his driving force.

He never saw that because he overspent, he'd not have enough money to pay bills or to live and once again he would expect me to give him mine. So in the end, he wasn't generous at all, I was, because I usually ended up paying for everything.

A few days after our daughter was born, I noticed that money had been taken out of my bank account. By now I knew who to suspect, so I asked him outright if he had taken it. He said no. He claimed that I must have taken it out and forgotten. I knew I hadn't, I hadn't been anywhere near a cash machine. Eventually, after an argument, he admitted that he had taken my card and the money. Can you imagine looking the mother of your children in the eye and lying so blatantly? I changed my pin number and started to get wiser about what I did with my purse.

I don't know if he didn't have the capacity to learn how to manage money, or if he simply didn't care how he got it, as long as he had enough.

My dad, who I recently found out had lent him far more money than I knew about, told me that he got to the point where he never expected to see any money he lent him again. My dad is a very generous man who cares for me and my children a great deal and I know that he took advantage of this. He used my dad's love of me and his grandchildren as a way to borrow money, claiming that it was for all of us and we needed it. It wasn't though, it was for him and his benefit alone.

I am very lucky that my dad is so amazing, because otherwise, this money could have ruined our relationship and I am very grateful that it hasn't, I know that he feels so disappointed and angry on my behalf for what I have been put through.

I have lost track of the amount of times I came down in the morning and money was missing from my purse. He took it without any consideration given to whether I needed it or not, and without a single thought about leaving me with nothing. He wanted it, he took it. I began to take my purse to bed with me so that he wouldn't have the opportunity to rifle through it whilst I was asleep.

He would get really aggressive if he borrowed money and I asked for it back. However, on the very rare occasions I needed to borrow money from him, I always asked. I also always paid it back quickly, but not before he harassed me with comments like "*Can I have that money back*", "*When are you going to pay me that money back?*" "*Have you got that money you owe me?*"

Now we aren't talking about hundreds of pounds, it was generally only a fiver, or very rarely twenty pounds. But he always got it back. I wouldn't dare behave this way to him, he would fly off the handle and the resulting argument would be far worse.

Eventually I had to take him off my credit card, because he would spend money and never pay it back, in fact, to this day, he owes me thousands of pounds just on credit card purchases alone.

I remember being really upset one year, when I found out that he had taken my credit card and bought my Mother's Day flowers with it. He hadn't asked, he hadn't told me, and he even initially lied about it when I asked. I'd have sooner gone without than increase the card balance. It was all show with him, he couldn't bear the thought that someone would criticise him for not getting me something nice from the children. It was never about making me feel special.

I can't remember when I started to hide money from him, but it was a number of years ago.

It didn't stop him though, he would go through my things and would often claim, when he finally admitted that he had taken it, that he had happened to find it by accident (even though it had been hidden maybe in a sock, right at the bottom of my underwear drawer), or that the tin it was in just happened to fall over and that's how he found it.

He found ways to overcome the access code to the digital money bank I had. He worked out how to use a knife or piece of card to get money out my money pots, and just took whatever he wanted.

I started writing down the amount I had, so that he couldn't claim that I had just forgotten how much I had.

There was never an apology or even awareness that he's taken something that didn't belong to him. That didn't register, it was in our home, therefore it must have been his to take.

He did admit later in our relationship that he didn't want me to have money, he felt that if I did, this would enable me to leave him.

I took on more and more work, meaning that I was teaching most weekends and spending several days a week doing marking and other admin tasks. There was even a time when I worked seven days a week for two or three months and I was exhausted. The work was good in that I was earning more, but the problem of him taking any money I had got so bad, that I started to lie about how much money I was earning. This way I could keep a rainy day fund.

He planned a surprise birthday party for me one year. My Mum and Dad contributed and he paid the rest, except afterwards he 'borrowed' money from me because he didn't have enough, so although he got the praise from others for doing such a lovely thing, essentially I paid for my own party.

As I said earlier, I'm not ungenerous, I'd always been happy to pay my own way, but there is a difference between being given a choice and having it taken from you. It's also having to put on a front for everyone else. No one knew what was happening behind closed doors, I was alone in this situation and often I was not only hurt by his actions but angry that I was essentially lying to our friends.

My grandad sadly passed away and left me some money. I had my eye on a bracelet, something I could remember Grandad by, but the money was spent covering debts he had run up.

When my mum died, she too left me some money and again, the money was spent covering debts.

My nan died, same story…

An inheritance, no matter how small should be used to have something to keep their memory alive, to do something worthwhile with. He took that from me. My family would never have wanted that.

We reached a point where I insisted that if we bought something, or went on holiday, that we each had to pay half. That worked for a while, at least it curbed his spending to some degree.

When I was going through chemo (you'll read about that later), not only did he not work, but he borrowed money from my family to pay the mortgage. It transpired that not only did he not pay the mortgage, but he bought a motorbike from someone he knew. Someone who over the following months kept knocking on my door looking for the money he was owed. That's how cold he was. If he could lie for his own gain then his didn't care who he sold out.

I think the one thing I will probably never forgive him for, is that despite our terrible financial situation, which he must have known about, he continued to smoke and drink every single day.

Even putting aside the fact that it was dangerous to mine and my children's, cigarettes as everyone knows, are expensive and he would regularly smoke thirty a day. Whilst when he was earning, it was his money and his choice, but when he wasn't working, had no money, and even owed money, never once did he even consider quitting.

He never gave a thought to the fact that the money he was spending on cigarettes and alcohol would have paid more than half of our mortgage each month.

We nearly lost our house because he missed so many mortgage payments. I had to go through the stress and humiliation of having to go through my income and outgoings with a stranger to prove I could pay the mortgage, and this on top of being just a few months out of chemo, nearly pushed me over the edge.

I thought the changes I had made would stop us being in the position of not being able to pay our bills, but it seemed it wasn't enough, so I had to take over paying everything because he simply kept spending money and never had enough to pay his share.

Money became such a huge issue, well maybe not to him, he always had enough, he just didn't care how he got it. I can't actually tell you how much he still owes me and my family and because of his inability to care or understand even the basics of money management, I'm now constantly driven by the need for reassurance that I can pay my way.

I went from the person I was, to rather a hoarder. I squirreled money away just in case. I felt sick if I had to spend money. I went without things, so that I would have enough for bills or to buy things my children needed.

Even now, some four years later, I still get anxious the day before the mortgage payment goes out. I check over and over that I have enough money in my account and it's like I can't breathe until I know the payment has gone.

If when reading this you think I come across as a bit resentful at times, I understand, and it's true, I really did get that way, but this was only after years of him, despite most of the time earning more than me, spending his money and then wanting to spend mine, even though I was already paying my share of the bills and more.

If there's one thing you take from this, don't get a joint account. If you already have one, then get yourself a separate account that no one else knows about, have your wages paid in there and set up a standing order, give the bank cards to someone you trust and don't leave them or money where they can be found.

Chapter 3
Life continued

To put it into context, I was never really happy back in the UK after working in Spain. I'd gone from a sunny climate with loads of friends, in charge of quite a large holiday site, to living back with my parents, no friends and pretty much no money. I yearned to go back, in fact, I remember when Jack was young, this was after I started working again, trying to work out if I could live with him in Spain most of the time and just come back for work. If I could have done, I would have, but then debts started piling up and my dream got further and further away from me.

I told him once, that many years before I had received an anonymous Valentine's card from someone claiming that they really liked me. I found it quite unsettling. You know what he did? He bought a new phone, in my name, I have since found out (it was easier then), and sent me an anonymous text telling me how much he liked me. He did confess and thought it funny. I didn't. This was just an example of his mind games. He would argue it was a harmless prank but it had the desired effect of keeping me unsettled.

I thought I could rely on him but even when Jack was born he messed up; it was a long forty eight hour labour, he was there with me, well most the time, but he very nearly missed the actual birth because he was outside smoking, no thought for what I was going through.

After we went home, life seemed pretty good and although money was tight, everything was okay for the most part.

I would sometimes see him driving his bus when I walked around our local town, or on my way to get Jack weighed and it always made me smile.

We saw my parents, or my sister, niece and nephew quite a lot and everyone got on with him. He would help them with anything if they asked. He wasn't quite as handy with the DIY as he thought, but he was quite mechanically minded and was always ready to lend a hand.

We moved into a flat when Jack was about a year or so old. I can't remember why we moved, maybe it was cheaper, but anyway, we weren't there that long when we moved again, this time to a house with a garden. We were close to my parents again and Jack spent one day a week with my mum.

He changed jobs, and although this meant we had to pay off the remainder of the cost for his bus driver training, something he seemed completely unaware that we needed to do, he was very much like that, never thinking about the repercussions but he seemed happy in his new job. He was earning more money and even though he was up early, he wasn't working shifts anymore and although I know that by this point money had definitely started disappearing from my purse on a regular basis, life just carried on and I felt reasonably happy and settled.

When Jack was about two and a half, I got pregnant, something we were both happy about. I was sick a lot and I definitely didn't feel as good as I had with Jack. However, about eight or nine weeks later, the sickness had disappeared and I was feeling good so went away for the weekend with some friends. It was a lovely break, until that is, I started to bleed and after a visit to the hospital, I found out that I had miscarried. It was horrible but he looked after me, made sure I ate and hugged me when I cried. I never saw him show any emotion about it, but put that down to him being a man and not showing emotion the way I did.

As I mentioned earlier, he would fly off the handle for no reason but the harder thing to deal with was him playing up when we had planned to go out . He'd kick off and say he wasn't going or cause a scene, often without any real discernible reason but in the end he would always go.

This put a strain on me as it often led to me feeling really anxious that either I would have to explain to others, or try and persuade him to go. I rarely enjoyed nights out because this had gone on before we left, I usually still felt anxious when we were there. I realise now that even then, I had started to get used to it.

An example that has stayed with me was his 40th birthday. I had planned a surprise dinner with my sister, brother in law and some of his friends. It was only a small thing, but then he didn't have many friends. Earlier that day I had taken a pregnancy test and although the line was very faint, it was definitely there. I told him this and he seemed happy.

As the meal progressed he drank more and more, and when we got to the end and we started to sort out the bill, he got really angry saying that we shouldn't expect the others to pay, that we should pay for it all. That isn't what had been arranged, no one else thought we should pay for it all, and it wasn't something I could afford to do.

He left the pub on his own, and when I got back to my sister's house, where Jack was staying with his cousins, the car was gone and so was he. He had abandoned us and just left.

I didn't sleep much, I was worried about him, anxious and quite frankly a bit embarrassed that he had behaved that way, and in public. The next day, after my brother in law drove us home, I found out that when he got home, he didn't have his door keys, so he kicked the door in.

Coincidence or not, the pregnancy came to nothing.

When Jack was about three, I was offered a job as a self-employed trainer for a hypnotherapy and counselling training school. I had qualified as a hypnotherapist a few years before I went to work in Spain, and as the teaching days were only at the weekend, it seemed perfect.

I did have to stay away one weekend a month, as the classes were too far for me to get to otherwise, but it worked well and he looked after Jack whilst I was away.

After getting over my initial nerves, I really started to love my job, it seemed that I had a talent for teaching, so I asked to have more responsibility. I was given additional teaching and marking work and as time passed, he encouraged me to take on more and more work.

I did get quite tired, looking after Jack, marking work and being available to students during the week and then working at the weekends but I figured that the more I earnt, the easier life would be, and yet we never really seemed to have much and what I had, I often ended up spending on his share of the bills.

During this period, his sister and then his dad died and I remember standing at his dad's funeral, when the grandmother of 'his' other child came over and starting talking to him about it. I just remember everyone looking at me and her being ushered away. My world really fell apart that day, because I had believed him when he said it wasn't his, yet the grandparents and his own family believed that he was the father.

Over the years he still claimed the child wasn't his, but I will tell you more about that later.

One day, years later, he told me that it was my fault he hadn't been able to mourn for his Father, because he had had to look after me at the funeral. He had no awareness of self-blame. I know now that he is most likely a sociopath.

We moved again, just after Jack had started pre-school, this time we were near to my sister, brother in law, nephew and niece and again, it was okay. I was working more and more, we had enough, but still never more than that.

About a year later we moved again, this time to Cambridgeshire, into a four bedroom house and whilst we were there, life was actually pretty good. We had friends, we threw parties, Jack was settled at school and despite him sometimes drinking too much I was starting to breath out.

We wanted our own house and to give him his due, he worked really hard for several months, did lots of overtime and made sure we had enough to qualify for a mortgage, which we did and we did buy our house, ironically, the one he drove into.

A few months after we moved in, I found out that I was pregnant, it was rather a shock, and if I am honest, I was really quite scared. I had had quite a bad time having my son and the thought of having to give birth again quite frankly terrified me. He wasn't overly supportive and just got quite angry and aggressive when, for the first few months, I struggled to cope with the idea of being pregnant again. It wasn't all bad though, I do remember him running me baths, cooking so that I would eat and I guess he was pretty well behaved in many ways during this time.

I can't remember when he first lost his job, but I don't think it was his fault, the company had lost some contracts and they had to make cutbacks. I did feel really sorry for him, as he had enjoyed the job, had a few friends and it was a huge disappointment for him when he had to leave. Luckily he got another one quickly, but it was then the beginning of the end in many ways, for reasons you will soon discover.

Then his drinking, moods, and behaviour all started to get much worse.

In the September of 2010, Abbi was born, and he was there with me. He actually was very helpful to me, but a few days after she was born, money went missing from my bank account, I asked him and he said no, he said that I must have taken it out and forgotten. I knew I hadn't and later he admitted that he had taken my card and taken the money out.

I remember one day, when my daughter was tiny, he got in a rage about something, I don't remember what, but he kicked in our front door. I remember sitting on the edge of my bed, cradling my baby and sobbing, I was so terrified that I had to call friends to help. We had to get a second hand door, again from a friend, because we didn't have enough money to buy a new one.

It's almost like a repeating pattern, a period of good followed by intense drama, maybe because my attention wasn't focused on him or maybe just because he needed to feel in control.

Even before we moved into the new house, we had started sleeping apart, his snoring was dreadful, made worse by the alcohol and I couldn't take care of Jack and work without sleep. But we moved from a four bedroom to a three and then Abbi was born, this meant that we didn't have a spare room, so he slept on the sofa. It was his choice to do this, but we often had to leave the lounge as he was asleep by 8.30-9pm.

Life carried on getting worse as the years passed. He was drinking every single day, he would pour a drink pretty much the minute he walked in from work, and start drinking quite early at the weekends.

We seemed to lurch from one problem to another, from one job to another, but despite this, I always updated his CV when he asked, I applied for jobs on his behalf, I supported him and felt for him when he lost job after job. It was never his fault and I believed that he was maybe just unlucky.

I guess over the years I just got accustomed, it just seemed how our life was meant to be, I still didn't tell anyone the full extent of what was going on, because I was embarrassed. I have this reputation of being a strong woman, and I guess I am, but what would people think of me if they found out that I was putting up with this behaviour, that I felt so trapped by my fear of losing my home and not having enough money to look after my children, that I would rather stay than go?

He took me to Edinburgh for my birthday in 2015, he had planned it himself, with some help from one of my friends and we had a good time. He was good company, didn't drink too much and didn't cause any arguments. It was the last time I can remember having a good time with him.

The Easter of that year we went away with some friends and he caused problems again. He drank a lot, caused a row about something or the other, threatened to go home and ended up sleeping in the car. We all felt very uncomfortable and he was in a lousy mood the next day, he ruined the whole weekend and had embarrassed me yet again.

About a month or so later, in April 2016, I was diagnosed with Anaplastic Large Cell Lymphoma. Whilst waiting for a diagnosis, after seven months of tests and finally a biopsy, I was in agony. Nothing they gave me helped, I could barely stand and I remember rocking as the pain was so bad, I couldn't cope. He was there with me when I was told and I had to start chemo the following month.

He was good, he took me to appointments, cooked for me, cleaned the toilet for the first time since I had known him and made sure that the children were looked after. Now if you would have asked me at the time, I would have said that I don't know how I would have got through it without him.

But he also took six months off to look after me, at least that is what I thought he did. I do remember that about five or so weeks into my chemo treatment, I started to run a temperature. If you don't know much about chemo, this can be a major problem, because it is likely to mean an infection and needs to be treated quickly. I remember it even now, I had got out of the bath and started to shiver but was so exhausted I couldn't be bothered to move, I hadn't even got dressed, and just had a towel wrapped around me.

Taking my temperature was a regular thing during treatment, so I took it and it was a bit high and then it kept getting higher, but I was adamant that I wasn't going anywhere, I just wanted to sleep. I don't really remember much of what happened, but I do remember him making a call to the hospital and telling me that I had to go in. You couldn't just turn up at hospital, you have to call, tell them the problem and then wait for them to tell you to go in.

I still didn't want to go, I was too tired, but my temperature kept going up, so I had little choice. I got to the acute treatment centre and was taken off to a room, sure enough my temperature was still raging and because of my allergy to penicillin I had to be given two different antibiotics, via two different drips at the same time. There were doctors and nurses everywhere and I'm certain I was in and out of consciousness. They talked about moving me to a ward, but I was really terrified, as it was highly possible that the infection was as a result of my previous stay in a ward, so the lovely senior nurse, who had recognised me from my last visits, promised to keep me there as long as she could.

It was terrible, I didn't really know what was going on, just that I felt dreadful and I remember turning to him and saying that I didn't want to do this anymore. And you know what, he had a go at me, he told me off for being selfish. I didn't have the energy to argue, but he left soon afterwards and when I later messaged him to say that I had been told I had Sepsis, I remember him saying "You can die from that."

I later found out that he had hadn't taken six months off, he had actually lost his job and had no work to go to. Don't get me wrong, I was very grateful at the time that he was there, although he rarely sat with me, or watched something with me, he just brought food, or whatever I needed and then disappeared back downstairs. He could have gone back to work after about 4 months, or at least tried to find a job because I was coping better with the treatment, yet he decided not to. I continued trying to work as best I could, despite horrendous side effects, terrible sickness and infection after infection.

I got the all clear in September 2016, but as I am sure you can understand, it is something that I still fear going through again, even years later and yet, one of his favourite things to throw at me was telling me that he hoped my cancer came back.

Any of my friends who smoked, never smoked near me, not since I had lymphoma, but not him, he would stand in the back door and smoke and would then get annoyed when I asked him to go outside because the smoke was blowing back into the room.

I don't think I ever forgave him for that.

Even now I wonder if it was something that I did, if I had done things differently, would our lives have been different?, But then I would recall how many times I did offer help, support and love him, how many times I made excuses and stood up for him, and how many times I excused his behaviour.

Writing this book has made me realise how bad it was. You might think I was stupid, but I honestly never realised how much he put me through.

I actually felt sick when I wrote this, because I finally realised that he had sexually harassed and attempted to blackmail me as well. I could have listed the ways right here, it seemed to make more sense though for you to read it in context throughout the book.

I've written this book because I hope to educate people as to how abuse can start and develop, how easy it is to fall for the lies and excuses, and why it isn't so easy to spot. I hope this book helps those who need to find the strength to get out, those who might be in danger of ending up in this position and I want to highlight the shortfalls of the British justice system.

I would like to make one point here, I know domestic abuse happens to men as well, and the reason I refer to women and women's abuse charities, is simply because I understand if from this perspective. The truth is, I just haven't spoken to enough male victims to be able to speak confidently on the subject.

I have taken some liberties with reference to the dates of some of the narrative, the events are true and did happen during this period of time, it's just that I can't remember specific dates.

I have changed names where appropriate.

Chapter 4
Sociopath

Did I really know the man I married? Was there more going on than I had ever even considered?

He seemed 'normal' and his behaviour was normal, at least some of the time, but looking back, I wonder if I actually married a sociopath.

It's funny really, I never considered that his behaviour was extreme enough to warrant a professional diagnosis. I just thought that he was moody, irritable, a liar and a thief. I mean, it's not like that wasn't enough, but since he has been in prison, and having had this possibility pointed out to me, I have done some research.

Whilst **I am not qualified** to make this, or any other diagnosis, I am really quite clear now, that his behaviour definitely fits within the parameters of antisocial personality disorder, sometimes called sociopathy.

It's not surprising that I didn't spot it, as it is suggested that only around 3% of the population, although around three times as many men as woman, have the condition.

When I looked at the list of symptoms, I knew that I could tick each and every one off, based on his behaviour:-

- **Disregard for right and wrong** - he never seemed to understand that it was wrong to steal, lie, threaten or manipulate people.

- **Persistent lying or deceit to exploit others** - he most definitely lied, a lot, and he used so many tricks in his arsenal to exploit me and my family.
- **Being callous, cynical and disrespectful of others** – he certainly seemed to lack any form or empathy and I do not believe he respected anyone.
- **Using charm or wit to manipulate others for personal gain or personal pleasure** – before I got used to his behaviour, he would use charm to manipulate me into believing would be okay.
- **Arrogance, a sense of superiority and being extremely opinionated** – he hated arrogant people, and yet he was arrogant himself, he thought he was better than most of his work colleagues and he had an opinion on everything. They were usually very fixed, never backed up with anything other than his belief and he did not like to be challenged.
- **Recurring problems with the law, including criminal behaviour** - he now has at least three convictions, is in prison, broken his bail conditions several times, broken his restraining order several times, stolen, harassed, stalked and used aliases.
- **Repeatedly violating the rights of others through intimidation and dishonesty** - he attempted to intimidate me and my son so many times we lost count. .He would threaten to take his son's possessions and break or damage them. He would threaten to take his things from him for weeks or even months at a time. He never saw this through and always gave up after a day or so, but the threats didn't stop for many years.

- **Impulsiveness or failure to plan ahead** – he would buy and sell our cars at the drop of a hat, would spend impulsively without thought or consideration that we might need that money for bills and he had no idea what his future would be like, he certainly never planned for it.
- **Hostility, significant irritability, agitation, aggression or violence** – he definitely ticked all of these, and on an ever increasing basis.
- **Unnecessary risk-taking or dangerous behaviour with no regards for the safety of self or others** - I think the number of times he swallowed pills and him driving his car into my house pretty much covers this.
- **Poor or abusive relationships** – he didn't have any good relationships with anyone that I knew of, at least not for the past ten years or so and he was most definitely abusive towards me.
- **Failure to consider the negative consequences of behaviour or learn from them** – he never learnt, he just kept doing the same things. I don't think he thought there would be consequences for his actions, he simply blamed others and expected them to pick up the pieces.
- **Being consistently irresponsible and repeatedly failing to fulfil work or financial obligations** – he was irresponsible with money and failed to pay his share on many occasions.

After finding the above list of the signs of a sociopath from the Mayo Clinic website I became convinced that I was right.

So where does this leave me?

If I look back at the behaviour from an analytical point of view I can see how everything he did was calculated and planned with his own end game in mind. He was a perpetual victim and so many people "conspired against him". Sadly I think that if he saw this, he would believe that it vindicated his actions and that he "wasn't to blame" as it was just the way he was created.

Let me give you some examples of how the behaviour manifested the traits above.

His "Other Child";

Get blood tests I said.

I did and they proved he isn't mine.

Get a copy of the results and we can prove it.

I would but there was a fire at the doctors surgery…

Find his mother and sort it out.

Don't know where she is.

Okay, seek legal advice.

He booked an appointment, and showed me the email confirmation. He even went to the solicitors, I sat outside the building. He claimed to go at least one further time, but I never saw an invoice from them. He claimed they were going to bill him after it had been sorted. Well I don't know of any solicitor who waits 15+ plus years to bill anyone and honestly, it got to the point where I simply gave up asking. To this day, I don't believe him, but after a while the battle just didn't seem worth the grief and aggression he directed at me.

The child, well last I was told, was in Australia, a fully grown adult by now of course, but nothing he could do about blood tests until he returned to the UK… What man doesn't want to accept his own child or be responsible for him? The continued lies, lack of care, empathy or belief he was doing anything wrong is very apparent here.

Manipulation

"*I'm not going and you'll have to tell them.*" I lost track of how many times he said this to me, how often I felt embarrassed at the thought of having to tell people that my husband was being like a small child and sulking about something or other.

"*You just go and I'll stay here…*" I am certain that he pretty much always went wherever it was, but only after he had caused a lot of upset.

"*I'm not going on holiday, you go…*" This used to really bother me, but eventually I found a way around it. Instead of worrying what he might say, I simply started booking holidays without him, and they were definitely more fun than those with him.

I lost count of the number of times he embarrassed me in public, by shouting at or arguing with someone because he didn't like what they said, or did, or how they behaved.

When he argued with my son, I even had to stand between them at times. He never wanted to be challenged, he hated it and he couldn't deal with it. His response was always to be aggressive and forceful, and if, on the odd occasion he would accept that he was wrong . He would never say "*Sorry, you're right, I got that wrong*", or anything that showed he really accepted it, it was more like "*Oh it's all my fault, it's always my fault*" like a sulky child, at the beginning I'd jump in to pacify him and calm the situation, but honestly, he never changed. It was like he had these standards or expectations of others, but he never told them what they were and so they could never get it right.

Bullying

He would often comment that I wasn't perfect and that I did things wrong as well. The difference between him and I though, I never thought I was perfect and I apologised when I thought I was in the wrong. Actually that's not quite true, for years I apologised even when I knew I wasn't wrong, just because it was easier and I wouldn't have to deal with his bad moods.

I did ask him many times, if he could tell me what I was doing that he didn't like, or that he wanted me to do instead, but he could never tell me. Not once, not even one single occasion could he tell me. He simply claimed that he just forgot about things. When I pointed out that what I did couldn't have been that bad if he had simply forgotten, he would get aggressive and tell me that he couldn't just come with up examples. He would then often get nasty and I would leave it.

But with my son it was different, I guess because he was smaller than him, and he didn't have the verbal capacity I did, he felt that he had the upper hand. It was like the biggest kid in the class trying to bully the smallest. Except in this scenario, the big kid just wasn't that clever and small one had me by their side. I would never let him hurt my son, but I did pay for standing up for him.

Mainly I paid by him ignoring me. He would decide not to talk to me, to give very limited answers if I did speak to him, or by literally just ignoring me and pretending that I hadn't said anything to him. This would go on for varying lengths of time, until I guess, he decided that it had gone on for long enough. At which point, he would often just start talking as if nothing had happened.

When I challenged him about this, which I did now and then, he would just say it was done and over with and there was no point talking about it. I warned him one day that at some point Jack would be bigger than him and he should be careful. And that day did arrive. He had broken his leg in an accident at work and with self- pity pouring out of every inch of him, he started again and he went on and on.

My son leaned on his leg and just looked at him. Jack didn't hurt him, but you could almost feel the words *"I'm bigger than you now"* float between them. He shut up and backed off.

After this, with him clearly realising that he could no longer control Jack, he would just launch his attacks on me instead. He would tell me all the things Jack had done, that I should deal with him, I should be the one to tell him, and he would threaten me with how he was going to "deal with Jack". He never did anything he said, but I felt every bit of his anger.

You know, writing this has reminded me that when Jack was younger, if he misbehaved, he would threaten to take him to social services. Jack would clearly get upset and I would again be stuck in the middle. I would never let Jack be taken, and I am sure that he never would have done it, firstly he had no grounds and secondly he was too lazy, but the damage was done. It actually makes me feel quite sick thinking about not just what he did over all these years, but that I didn't do something.

It probably seems obvious now, obvious that I should have done something, but I honestly didn't see that I had many, or rather any options. I made sure that my son was safe, and I guess that I hoped that if I loved him enough, that he would change. Given that we could go for weeks or months and everything was okay, I think I learnt to kind of forget how bad it was when it was bad. It never occurred to me that this was abusive behaviour. He just got moody, could be nasty and that's just how he was. I got used to it.

Lying

As I mentioned earlier, he lost his job time and again, I think we got to around eight or nine jobs he lost in total. He either failed his probation, was sacked, or jumped before he was pushed. Always for the same reasons, he knew better than everyone else, and he wasn't quiet in pointing this out. He moaned and complained to me almost every single day about people at work. They were all useless, they didn't know what they were doing and he was the only one who did. I suggested more than once that perhaps if he kept his mouth shut, and worked to get promoted, that he could make changes from within, but no, he wouldn't do that, so as these 'idiots' got promoted he didn't.

I actually got to the point where I stopped asking what his day was like, because I knew he would start moaning and complaining about everything and everyone. Not that this stopped him though, he told me anyway.

For my own sanity, I am glad that I have lost track of the number of times he threatened suicide (always my fault of course), for reasons that made no sense, if he even gave me a reason, which he often didn't. The smashed in front doors (two), smashed in when he was in a rage about something. The dented white goods and internal doors with holes in them where he punched them because he felt like it. The number of times he held his fist just an inch or two from my face or stood and looked at me with absolute hatred because he was angry about something I had done, or perhaps not done 'something', or simply because I wouldn't get out of his way. I had never seen before.

One of the difficulties I had was that I often had no idea what triggered his behaviour. He could go from being perfectly okay to raging within seconds and I just didn't know why. Would it have been different if there had been a pattern, or if the same thing triggered him off? I don't know. But I do know that rage that seems to come from nowhere and for no apparent reason is really hard to spot.

Times had been challenging now and then I guess, but nothing that could have led me to expecting punching and smashing things and he could never really give me any sort of reasonable or logical explanation either. I don't know if he didn't want to admit he had a problem, or if he just didn't know.

I learnt though, I learnt not to back down. So much so, that for the last couple of years, if he stood in my face, I stood in his. No matter how much I was bloody well shaking, or how close his fist came to my face, I would not back down, it was the only way I could deal with it.

The sulking, not speaking, poor me, it's all my fault (but not really) attitude, just got worse, although the not speaking to me became a blessing in the end, because I didn't have to listen to him moaning and complaining.

It wasn't just the sulking though, he lied, a lot and I do mean a lot, about anything and anyone. I don't know whether he did it to control others, to make himself look better, or to make them feel bad, not that he would say anything to people's faces, except mine or Jacks of course. No, he would talk about them but never confront them for these 'crimes' he seemed to think they had committed. He even once claimed that his Dad had kicked him so hard that he broke a rib. Since he was arrested, I have spoken to his family and no one has any knowledge of him ever having a broken rib.

He had no friends and resented that fact that I did. "*It's alright for you*" he told me, "*You've got friends*".

"*You're right*", I would say, "*But that's because I am nice to people, because I make an effort and am fun to be with.*"

He claimed his GP thought he had cancer, but there was never any evidence of hospital appointments or blood tests and when I didn't really react, basically because I'd heard it all before, he verbally attacked me for not saying, "*It's ok, we'll get through this together*", as he claimed he had when I was diagnosed.

There are two main reasons I am so certain that he never had anything wrong with him, one, I never saw a hospital letter and having received a lot, I knew what they looked like and he never asked me to order or collect his prescription, something he had done for years for the tablets he did take.

Not a week went by without him claiming to be ill in some way shape or form. He was overweight, drank and smoked too much and did pretty much no exercise. Even when he broke his leg, he never did the exercises he was given to strengthen it.

Alcohol

When we were first together, he drank, but not to excess and mainly at weekends.

Over the years this increased, until the point that he was drinking every day, not just a glass of wine, but a bottle or more every time.

He often walked in from work and before he even took his shoes off, he would pour a glass of wine, and more often than not, he would then start moaning and complaining about his day, his job, the people he worked with, his boss, or anyone else who had annoyed him.

When I worked at the weekends, I was usually home between 6 – 7pm and it was quite common that by the time I arrived, he was into his second bottle of wine.

He could quite easily, and often did, drink a bottle of vodka and two or three bottles of wine over a weekend.

I did ask him if he thought he maybe had a drink problem, but he always denied it and got aggressive. He even said he would quit on a few occasions, but he never lasted for more than one day.

I am sure that he must have driven whilst over the limit on probably hundreds of occasions over the years but it just never seemed to bother him.

The drinking was bad enough, but the rages, usually stemming from the alcohol, were even worse.

Rages

I can't remember the first time he flew into a rage, but I know that he could go from calm to raging in seconds and often with no warning.

I do know that I used to be really scared when he did this and I spent years being the peacemaker, being the one to speak to him and try to resolve things. But even so, he would often go for hours or even days not talking to me and this used to really bother me. I am a proactive person, if there is an issue, I like to resolve it and move on, but his behaviour didn't allow for this.

It wasn't just aggressive language either, he was violent as well. He would smash things, throw things about, threaten me and sometimes my son.

As I've said, over the years, he smashed in two front doors, punched dents in the fridge and draining board, punched holes in at least two internal doors, smashed any number of plates and glasses. He threw my sons phone in the bath whilst I was in it, smashed his sons wardrobe, and frequently threatened to smash his property.

I am surprised that both our back door and front door survived, given the number of times he slammed them shut in anger.

Thinking about it, he never did anything that would actually cause himself any harm, he only hit or broke things that either belonged to someone else, or would leave a lasting visual impression on the rest of us.

It wasn't just us that felt his rage. I remember being on holiday once and he kicked off for some reason or another, shouting, swearing and threatening one of the Reps. It was so bad that the hotel threatened to call the police, several other guests complained and the next day a letter was slipped under our door saying that the holiday company was withdrawing their Rep Service from him, not us, just him.

He just would not accept any responsibility and I think the hotel agreed that we could eat in our rooms, because I was both embarrassed and worried about what he might do next.

Eventually I did give up trying to play peacemaker and I actually ended up enjoying the peace when he wasn't talking to me. In a way I even looked forward to him kicking off, because I would simply walk away and I knew I could likely expect a few days of peace from him.

I don't think he knew what to do when I met his silence with silence, he wasn't getting the reaction he wanted and I think it threw him a bit. It didn't stop him, but at least I no longer felt the fear and anxiety that had become my norm.

If it was that bad, why didn't I leave?

A simple question, not a simple answer, but I will attempt to explain. -

When you are a good person, a caring person, you tend to forgive easily, create explanations, fall for apologies and just think the best of people. Periods of happiness and calmness lead you into a false sense of security.

Not to mention the children, the threats of no money, the debts, the fear of losing your home, the questioning of your own mind, the wondering if you are to blame, if you made it worse or if you are making it out to be worse than it is. Actually a few people gently pointed out to me, after he left, that I shouldn't downplay what he had done to me, that he had put me through hell.

You normalise someone's behaviour when things happen gradually. It is amazing what you can get used to, or what becomes the norm when it is drip fed or comes in waves. And that's what I did, I got used to it. He just had a temper, he got frustrated, he couldn't manage money, he really did love me, he really did regret it after he threatened me or smashed things.

But of course he didn't really, he just was rather adept at controlling me and the situation. Now I am a reasonably intelligent woman, a therapist for heaven's sake, but you know what, I never saw it. I never saw it until someone told me what he had been putting me through was domestic abuse. And my God, I felt really bloody stupid when I realised.

Did I leave then?

No.

Why?

Because the pressure was unbearable, the doubts kicked in, the fear of having to go through what I knew would happen when I told him was just too much.

But really, it didn't take too many more months before I did tell him to leave. End of story? No, not even close.

Leading up to this I was accused of having an affair, not once but several times. He didn't like me going out. Oh he never just came out and said it, no, he just tried to cause arguments before I went out hoping to spoil my evening. On one occasion I even offered to send him a photo of where I was and who I was with to prove to him I was with female friends.

Then one day, I had reached the point where I had had enough. In some ways it was simpler than I expected, in that he agreed to move out. Actually he suggested it, something I never thought he would do, at least not so easily. For me, I had just reached the end of wanting to deal with or cope with him and his behaviour any longer. There were things that pushed me to this point, things you will read about, but I guess, at the end of the day, I just didn't want him in my life anymore. ,

Once he had gone, I thought that would pretty much be it, the end, but it wasn't.

This is what I was up against:-

"And just so you know, I've got a gun in the car cos that's how bad I feel about this."

I didn't believe him, not at first, he had lied so much and honestly him having a gun just seemed so far out of what I expected my 'normal' life to be, that it just seemed ridiculous.

"Show me" I said

"No, I'm not getting it out, or I'll take us all out. I'm not just leaving you or me behind."

Now I started to get scared. I couldn't really form any words in my mind, I actually remember sitting on my bed sort of mute, because I just didn't know what to say. But as the confusion and fear began to take shape, he followed with;
"Don't worry, I won't shoot you in your sleep, you'll see it coming and you'll know why."

There was no gun, but the damage was done.

Let's go back just a little way, to March 2019, which is before we split up.

Chaper 5
Life As I Knew It

March 2019

31st

So you get your boobs out for
Facebook but not for me.

All I had done was post a photo. I had never really liked having my photo taken, but I felt really happy and actually liked the picture, just a simple selfie, taken in my bedroom, so I posted it.

No, I thought I looked pretty in
the photo, that's why I posted it,
nothing 2 do with my boobs,
but I've changed it now.

Thanks for trying to make me
feel bad.

My boobs weren't out, you could simply see some cleavage.

I did later re-post it because I didn't see why I shouldn't post something that I was happy about.

April 2019

1st

It was not meant that way it
was meant to be a joke

And that's why there
was no smile, no wink
and you went off 2
bed without speaking??!!

What was this about? I have no idea, but I suspect it was his way of backing out of his comment about me 'getting my boobs out' for Facebook.

4th

I was really tired of it all. I had gotten to the point where I didn't think I could really feel much of anything anymore, I just wanted it to stop. I wanted the crazy mood swings, ignoring me, lying to me, stealing money and plain and simple daily negativity to stop.

We clearly aren't getting on,
neither of us is happy so
what shall we do about it?

I don't know yet will have to
think about it

Ok, well please let me know
when you have thought about it
I would prefer to discuss via text/
messenger for the time being
rather than in person as I don't
want to deal with any aggression.

Ok

Have you given this any thought?

Several hours had passed and as I hadn't heard anything from him, which was quite unusual, so I asked him directly if he had given the situation any thought. The reason I asked him, rather than giving my thoughts and opinions first, was so that he couldn't later blame me and tell me that it was all my idea.

A little have you

Of course.
What are you thinking?

I should move out

I think that's a good idea.
Are you thinking trial separation
or permanent?

I need to get some money together
and find some place I can afford
then see what happens

Which was never going to happen, as he never had any money.

I asked him once if he had a drug or gambling problem, as I simply could not work out how he always had so little money. He denied it, but it was going somewhere.

6th

That's if I'm still alive you know
this is end for us

That is your decision.

Best you stay away til Monday
and if you find me dead then I
hope it haunts you for the rest
of your life

Why didn't I answer him? Because over the years I had honestly lost track of how many times he had threatened to kill himself, and each and every time, it was my fault.

It happened so many times, I'd wrestled pills and whiskey out of his hands, cutting myself trying to get the packet away from him. I'd emptied the house of any drugs that had been left over after my chemo treatment, after on one occasion he took all the morphine that I had left in a bottle. He never hid away or genuinely attempted to take his life, it was always in front of me, or at least documented by text and photo.

These incidents were often preceded by an argument, or him threatening me in some way, to the point that I even grabbed a knife on one occasion he scared me so badly.

I stayed out as much as possible and spent a night with my daughter at a friend's house, because if I had gone home I know I would have been subjected to more grief and abuse. I couldn't stay the next night as she had family arriving so I went to another friends for the day, finally to receive a text saying –

You can come home,
I'm going to bed.

I went home, but left again less than five minutes later because the minute I walked in he came downstairs and the abuse started.

"I'm going to kill myself and it will be on your conscience."

"I hope your cancer comes back and you have no one to look after you."

"This is the last time you are going to see me."

He said to our, then eight year old daughter.

And it went on and on until I could get my daughter back out of the house. We had nowhere to go. Honestly, I was too embarrassed to go to my family, so my daughter and I had to stay in a hotel for the night. Funnily, our night away, sat in bed, eating pizza and watching Benidorm on my iPad is one of her favourite memories and she often asks me if we can do it again.

The next day he moved out.

The end? Nope, still not close, months of begging and harassment followed…

8th

This has made me really sick I'm coughing up blood and there is even blood in my stool and nose I am sorry it has come to this I hope you find a better place once I have gone.

I had no idea if he was really sick and I can only guess that he meant moving out had made him feel this bad.

Just to let you know this has ripped my heart apart I have not even got to see Abbi and Jack to say goodbye whatever happens between us please tell them that I will always love them.

I'm sorry its come to this as well but I tried so hard, I asked you to seek help, I asked you to come with me, I asked you to stop being so angry and aggressive. I really wanted you to help me help us but for whatever reason it didn't happen.

Maybe I shouldn't have replied to his messages, but despite the fact that I did not want to be with him, did not want to even see him, didn't mean that I wanted him to be in pain and suffering. We had been married a long time and he was the father of my children. It would have felt wrong to just ignore him, although perhaps that is exactly what I should have done.

I had been asking him for years to seek help, but he always said that he would sort it out his own way.

I asked Abbi if she wanted to see
you but after Saturday evening
she said no. I will always tell them
you love them, I have no interest in
making you into a villain, so please
don't let them down.

I have got here this is a right shit
hole piky galore I'm going to see
if I can get a hotel

He had made no effort to find anywhere. He refused the first couple of places I found, but I sent him the details of this place, a caravan site and he agreed to it. I paid the deposit, which was wasted as he left and he never once offered to return it to me.

I honestly wouldn't let a dog stay here
I would rather sleep in my car
this is really the pits please
don't let me live like this
Please help me
I'm begging you please

I offered help, but he didn't want anything I suggested.

...I'm just going to disappear best
for everyone I'm sitting here
crying my eyes out

Never, and I do mean never, in the 17 years I had known him had I seen him cry. Not when his kids were born, when I had a miscarriage, when is sister and then his dad died, not when I was diagnosed with lymphoma, or when I could have died from sepsis, never did he show true, genuine emotion towards or about anyone.

9th

Can we try and resolve this
situation I'm sure we can
this is costing us money we
don't have can you bring
yourself to let me come home
even if it's only for a few weeks
till we can get some funds together
and I can if you still want me to
move out I can get something
better so at least the children
can come and see me

You can't put that on me. I didn't
do this lightly and I can't/won't
risk you abusing me again, you
have no idea of the damage it
has caused to me. The only way I'm
prepared to try is if you stay away
and we seek professional help, I'm
sorry but I just can't cope with
it anymore.

My biggest problem is that I have
asked and asked and begged you to
seek help and you wouldn't.
Now I've finally been pushed here,
suddenly you want to sort it out.
Why didn't you love me enough to
seek help b4 this point???

I'm sorry I know I should have I
really don't want to loose you
and my family

I'm not sure that we are going to
do anything here other than go
round and round at this. I am
trying hard not to bring up
everything you have done because
I have tried to forget most of it.
I need time to sort out how I feel,
and although you probably won't
want to hear this, I spoke to a
solicitor a while ago to see where
I stood, and legally your behaviour
is seen as domestic violence.
Can you imagine how fucking
stupid I felt not to have seen that?
How I felt to discover my husband,
the man I loved so fucking much I
couldn't even consider my life
without him in it had been abusing
me for years? I need time, I'm sorry
but I need time on my own first and
I need to see you are genuine, with
looking out for children
financially etc.
Jack hates me and that is not my
fault.

Ok will you at least help me find something better than this so at least I can see the children. I am truly sorry for this and believe me this is not ideal for me out of any other relationships I have had I never ever thought this would happen to us I am crying just now saying this once again I am truly sorry and I am begging for your help.
I can just about except that its over between us but not being able to see Jack and Abbi is destroying me just to let you know I did try to top myself on Saturday I took all the sleeping tablets that I had only 16 but didn't work if you could call that site and find out maybe I could buy a caravan and put it there at least if they wanted to see me they could possibly stay like a camp out.

I couldn't help feeling concerned and more than a little confused. He wanted the children to stay, something I wouldn't have stopped, except, if he was going to keep trying to kill himself, or at least claim to, how did I know they would be safe? How could I be certain that he wasn't going to attempt something, or claim he had when my children were there? And I found it hard to comprehend how you can go from I'm feeling destroyed and have taken tablets to can you call and see if I can buy a caravan so the children can camp out with me??

I ended up speaking to my Dad and he agreed to let him stay at his house. I really wish I hadn't as he was only a couple of minutes away and had easy access to us.

12th

Hello can this week get anymore
worse my car has broken down
keeps going into limp mode know
you asked if I had a leak well yes
it's a diesel leak from my car it
runs for a bit then looses fuel
pressure then goes into limp mode
for about 10 miles then does it
twice last night on way back and 3
times this morning on way to work
having a real shit week.

A phone call followed with more complaints and guilt trips.

13th

You think I have no emotions
Jack just called me and I couldn't
speak to him because I started
crying.

I know but you didn't show any when
we were 2gether.

I'm trying not to get frustrated
but I hate this and I hate myself
for getting to this I have been
trying to be positive.

It will get better but it will take time. This has hurt me 2 but I couldn't take any more, sorry. If you want to make a better life, you can.

Not without you I won't

If you're honest you weren't happy with me, you can't have been or you would behaved differently.

No this has actually made me feel how much I do love you.

How am I meant to respond to that? Don't you think you should have worked this out at some point in the past 17 years?

I have always loved you and
probably always will have only
just realised how much I know
I have taken you for granted
this mas made me realise I have
to change and believe me if it's
what I have to do to get you back I will

You can only change for you, not me.
It's not my right to ask you to
change, only you can decide that.
Seek help, sort your shit out
and we'll talk but I can't promise
anything, sorry

Does that mean you don't love me
is over between us.

It means sort yourself out and
we'll talk. I don't love how it's
been for a long time and there
is absolutely no way I'm ever
going back to that. But if you
change because YOU want to, then
maybe there's a way forward but I
can't know that yet.

I want to do the right thing
because I love you and the
kids so much I want us to be
a family and a happy family
not seeing any of you has
made me realise how much
of an arse I have been and I'm
willing to do whatever it takes
to get this all sorted out.

Then I will give you the name and
number of a counsellor, go sort it
out and prove you love us, even on
days when you are pissed off. I need
a man who is loving, supportive,
proud of me, who respects me and
who I can talk 2 about ANYTHING
without him getting angry or
aggressive or making it about him.
I have learnt to shut up so as not to
have to deal with this and that will
never happen again.

Send me the details and I will go
I have even come into work
because I hate being on my own

Please don't try and make me
feel guilty.

I'm not trying to make you feel bad
I'm just telling you how I feel and
how much I miss you and the kids

I feel as if I lost you a long time ago.
You went from the man who
comforted me, who I trusted,
who told me everything would be
alright to a liar, a thief and someone
I couldn't trust. That hurt more than
you'll ever know. Not trying to make
you feel bad, just trying to tell you
how much I feel I've lost.

Believe me I want you to trust me
and love me like before I know it
may take time for you and I'm
trying to sort out and want to
sort it out.
So does that mean you are going
to look for someone else

No it doesn't mean that

Sorry just the way you said it made
it look like you where going to be
looking or already found someone
sorry for thinking that you do
mean the world to me.

He just wouldn't accept it was about him, he wanted me to have found someone else, so that he could blame them and me and it wouldn't be his fault.

I have messaged counsellor to for
an appointment.

Not got anyone, not looking for anyone but not sitting in house waiting. I've lost enough of my life through illness. I have friends, male and female and I will be going out and spending time with them. If something happens for you and me it could only be on grounds that I am allowed to be who I am because after many years of working on myself, I love who I am now.

So what you're saying is it is ok if you meet someone else I'm confused.

Not saying that at all, just saying I'm going to have a social life and not just sit in biding my time.

Sorry I have never stopped you from having a social life I only want to know if there's a chance you and me can sort this out or is it me just being wishful if you are saying it's over between us then I will just have to let you go.

I know but you've also given me silence and accused me of having an affair. There's more than 1 way to stop someone doing something. I've told you several times now, sort yourself out and we'll talk. I'm not saying there's no hope but not going to make false promises by guaranteeing anything. Sorry, that's the best I can offer just now.

Have you de friended me on Facebook

If I had we wouldn't still be able to use messenger.

Ok last time I will ask in your heart of hearts would you like us to work this out I am going to take them bowling in Cambridge tomorrow then go for lunch if it's ok with you.

I think I've answered this as best I can already.

Yes that's fine for 2mrw.

I cannot give you a guarantee but if you'd rather I say it's totally over so you can move on then just say.

I have booked the bowling for

12.30 so will get them 11.
I have booked appointment with
counsellor for Tuesday after
Easter.

My son thinks I am in the wrong and
that I left his Dad

It upset me that my son told me that he thought I had been wrong to end it. He was feeling really angry and whilst I could understand it, it hurt that after finally doing the right thing of ending it, that this had caused more upset.

Apparently I'm wrong cos I left
you. It seems you both think I'm
wrong.

I have not said your wrong.

So you think I was right?

Why did it matter what he thought? It didn't but I was feeling very isolated and alone, very few people knew what had happened and I guess I wanted some reassurance, even from him! Makes no sense I know, and I certainly wasn't regretting my decision. Truth be told, I just wanted each of us to move on and find new lives with other people, but my confidence was flagging and so was my emotional energy and I felt so frustrated that I guess I wanted confirmation I had done the right thing.

Sorry don't know where this has come from.

What him or me?

Both I'm only doing what I can to try and resolve this

I have been trying for years to resolve all this bloody aggression but it's a bloody thankless task and I'm totally knackered.

14th

Is Abbi ok now she was quite upset when I had to go.

She was quiet when she got home and there was a few tears but she was fine after that . I told her you love her and she can see/speak to you when she wants.

How is Jack

Quiet initially but he is speaking to me now which is an improvement on yesterday.

15th

Counsellor has got back to me to confirm my appointment is she the same one you see.

Yes. I will probably stop seeing her though whilst you are so there's no cross over.

All I was going to say was do you want me to give her permission to let you know what I have been saying if there's anything up I am looking to go on Tuesday evening.

No it's fine, they're your sessions they should be private between you and her. That way you can be honest in a safe space.

I know that but was just trying to help you if there was thing you many want to know it may help you if you know does that make sense to you.

That's fine, if you want to give her permission. She may suggest it's not the best thing but feel free to give it if you feel it may help.

I'm asking you if it will help I
want to help you as much as me sorry
didn't mean it how it sounds but I
think you know what I mean you know
I'm not as good with some words but
I think you know what I mean.

I've not taken it badly or
negatively, I'm just not sure
if/how it will help. But you can
give her permission then if
something comes up and she needs to
share then fair enough.

I'm only trying to help
how are you feeling

Tired, numb, happy, sad

If I can help you I will

It's up to them and you

I will see them whenever they want
to see me

Ok. I know Abbi is planning on
seeing you Wednesday evening.

Yes you said earlier I just don't
like her getting upset

Oh sorry, brain is fuzzy I forget
what I'm saying she will get upset
every time for the time being but
the only other option is to not let
her see you and that won't help I
don't think.

I want to see them as much as
possible I miss them
I'm sorry I didn't want to say it in
the same sentence I miss you more
Just to let you know Jack actually
asked me for a hug on Sunday

He asks me for
a hug now and then.

Have you got plans with them for
the weekend

No, nothing planned at the
moment.

I wish I could give you a hug.
I'm sorry I will try and not tell
you how I'm feeling

16th

It's not that I don't care, but I've become rather numb over the years and I need time to come alive again.

Would you like me to see if I can take them away for the weekend.

Sorry but I don't think I am ready to see you yet

Sorry, misread that!

It's up to you and them

I will have a look and see

He didn't.

Abbi will probably say yes and Jack will probably say no but you can try

Or they can just visit you at Dads and maybe go out for the day?

Can Abbi have dinner with me tonight

If she wants to

She says yes

Ok

17th

Abbi would like to stay with me tonight is it ok she is very sad and upset also if it's ok with you she would like to stay at the weekend as well

I later asked Abbi if she had been okay when she saw her Dad. It was all very new for her and I just wanted to check that she was okay, didn't have any questions and was dealing with everything. She told me she was fine, she never mentioned being sad or upset and said that he had asked her if she wanted to stay.

She can stay 2night but I'm working in the morning so she needs to be back by 9.45am. If you don't mind I will talk to her tomorrow about weekend cos I'm not sure staying all weekend will help as then she will be more upset when she can't see you every night?

I had made it really clear to him and our children that I wasn't going to prevent them from seeing him or make it difficult for him to see them. I was however mindful that emotions were high and I wanted to make sure that normal life was maintained as much as possible, at least until everyone had gotten used to this new situation.

Ok thank you she is coming to get her blanket and jammies.

Ok

Will you let me know that she is ok later on please

Of course

Thank you

Abbi is fine she is going to sleep with me

Ok thank you

19th

Hello how are you

I'm ok thank you

That's good is it ok if I take Abbi to get her Easter egg

Of course. Jack told you what I've already got hasn't he?

Yes I didn't just want to take her without you knowing

Thank you.

The guy from Wyton got back to me this morning he is decorating and cleaning it at the moment and said it should be ready next week to go and see it.

A nice, local residential caravan site I had given him the number for.

That's good. Jack mentioned that he'd been in touch and you were going to see it.

He never went to see it. I asked him a few hours after he had been booked to see it, if it was okay and he told me that he never went. I asked him why and he told me that the guy was busy and he would make another appointment. I asked a few days later if he had heard anything, he said no and there seemed little point in me asking again, as it seemed clear to me that he had no intention of going.

Can Abbi have her egg just now it's only a small one

That's fine

Can Abbi have dinner here with me

If she wants to which she will, so yes ok

As I say I would rather ask you first

Thank you

I am wanting to do this the correct way so that we can try and get on with each other.
Sorry I have just checked my account he standing order has not come out yet I will check again in the morning could be because of bank holiday but I think bank is open tomorrow if so I will go in and transfer it over but if it does come into your account after bank holiday can you transfer it back.

I appreciate it. No problem and yes of course I will.

Just to let you know I'm still having trouble with my wages only got £698 this week.

That's stupid, have you spoken to them?

Maybe you need to look elsewhere?

I will do on Tuesday yes but not going to get anything paying much more than 35k

What about another contract job? I take it you not taking one in Scotland?

No point that only pays 37.5k

This may seem like a decent wage, but that does depend on where you live and your outgoings, that and the fact he had been earning around £42,500 in his previous job, then it was quite a drop.

Fair enough, don't blame you then.

I can understand that people might think that we were obsessed with money, given how often it is mentioned and they'd be right to some extent. Money was a major issue and it came up when there wasn't enough, when he stole it, when he lost one job and was looking for another, when debts had to be paid off and on any other number of occasions. So obsessed maybe, but for me at least it was a way of trying to ensure that we had enough to pay for the things we needed.

Do you think there is a chance soon that we can meet up for a coffee and

a chat face to face the anger of all
this has gone now and I think we
could talk.

Ok

Thank you you can decide
when and where

I really don't mind but nowhere
public cos don't want people
listening

Well do you want to come over to your
dads

If you want but no kids there

Well you will have to sort that bit
out

What do you mean?

What to do with them

They'll have to be at home. When do
you want me to come over?

When ever you want to I don't want
you to feel any pressure just when
you feel comfortable about doing it

Is Dad there now?

Yes

When is he going out?

Not sure why

Cos I will come later when he's out

What about kids

Well I assume Abbi coming home after
dinner and Jack will be home as far
as I know.

Or wot if I come round to you while
the two of them are here.

When?

I can come over now if you want
So do you want me to come over

Give me 10 mins

Looking back at this conversation now, I can clearly see the control, he wanted it on his terms and where he wanted it to happen.

We talked about what we should do next. He told me that he was going to get help and that he meant it this time. I told him that if he wanted help he needed to do it for him and not me. He told me that he loved me and didn't want to spend the rest of his life without. I told him that I was very sorry, but that I didn't feel the same. I told him that if he did change and I meant really change, that I wouldn't close the door on our relationship, but that I could not and would not put up with dealing with the same behaviour for the rest of my life.

The whole conversation was amicable and friendly to a huge extent I guess. It always threw me a bit when he was 'nice', because it reminded me of the man I married and I admit that it confused me and gave me pause to consider whether I had made the right decision. Maybe I was lazy, maybe I was a coward, but honestly, if it could have been resolved I most likely would have carried on, because I didn't want to believe that my marriage was ending, despite the pain it had caused me.

Can Abbi stay
I asked Jack he said no
Thank you for seeing me

That's ok, I just want to be happy

I want you to be happy to and
I would like to be the one that
makes you happy
It was really nice talking to
you today.

You're welcome.
I am actually very good company!

I really mean what I said today every
ther relationship I had in the past
wen its went wrong I have run away
from it and yes I nearly did it again
but it took me 35 years to find the
right one so no I'm not going to run
away from this one I'm going to
do my damdest to get it back
even if it takes time.

That's nice to hear

I really do mean it

I'm glad you are feeling good
and I really want it to continue

As I said earlier I do love you
And it was really nice to
give you a hug

20th

Hello good morning do you have any
plans for today or tomorrow since
we are getting on at the moment and
possibly from now on would you like
me and you to take the kids out for
the day maybe Thorpe Park and have
a picnic since it's going to be nice.

It seems a bit soon but if both
children want to go, I will go as well.

Sorry meant to say Drayton manor
do you want to ask Jack and let me
know before I say anything to Abbi
I just think it might be nice as we
have always done something
nice at easter

He doesn't want to go

It's too late now as tickets
had to be booked.

Look I'm not prepared to rush
anything between us but as we not
going there now, how about you and
me take Abbi out for an hour or so?

That would be great

I can be ready for about 10.30

Ok I will send her back now do you
want me to pick you up or do you
want to meet me here.

Ok and we'll walk back to you.

Can I sneak over and see you

Not just yet

I know was being hopeful
Do you want to meet upstairs
before you go

Sorry, I've already said no.

I got home safely

How did we get from everything being over to messages of love? You want the truth? I don't know. We did spend some time together and it was like it had been when we were first together. It was easy, comfortable, familiar and somehow it just seemed easier to see the good in the relationship and not the bad.

Despite everything, I still wanted it to be okay and I let myself see the elements that were.

That's good I don't want you
to hurt yourself
I have really enjoyed today
love you

I have enjoyed it 2

I hope that when you go to sleep
tonight you will dream about me

I know I will dream about you
my sweetheart
<Blowing kisses sticker >
I have really enjoyed holding you

I have missed that

To be honest with you so have I we
should be doing that more often

I agree but I think we need to keep
it just between us as we move forwards.
Don't want to move 2 quickly and just
paint over the cracks.

I know I want us to sort this out once
and for all and by the way I really
wanted to fling you onto the bed
earlier and kiss you
I hope you did then at least you still
have got feelings for me and that's
a good thing

I'm just very conscious that if we
push to quickly you might think that
you don't need counselling and that
we will just fall back into the old,
which I really don't want.

No I have decided I need to go to
counselling I actually want to go
and to be honest not for you
but for me
I has took me a long time to do
this but I need to do it for me
Let's not end today on a negative
it's been a fantastic day and I have
really really enjoyed the time
with you

I don't think it's negative,
I think it's honest and we need that

I've enjoyed today as well and I've
enjoyed being with you more today
than I have in a very long time

I totally agree with you and I hope
that we are being honest with each
other and yes I feel the same as you
I felt really close to you today and
hope that will continue

I'm just about to go to bed I am gong
to bed really happy I feel like you I
don't want to paint over the cracks
or even fill them I want to sand
them down so that they will go away forever
I know I keep saying it
but I really do love you –

Good night,
see you in the morning xx

<Smile sticker >
Good night my sweetheart
see you in the morning sleep well
You do know I could easily keep
talking to you

I'm not stopping you

I know but I don't want you to
get fed up with me

Trust me I'll tell if you do

This reminds me of when we first
met and I went off working and we
would text each other all the time

Yeah and I kept running out of
credit, cost a flippin fortune lol

But it was great texting

True. Weirdly we've had some our
best times texting

I know how strange
I actually wish you were here

I wish I was there too my next
text to you was actually going
to say good night as I was really
wishing that I was with you

I'm not really sure what to say now

Just say what you feel I am

But I did, I said I wish you were here

I will be there whenever you want me to be

You can come over and say goodnight

I'm coming over to see you

I will unlock the door. Just be quiet don't want Jack to hear.

I'm not going to lie, it was nice to have some attention, but a part of me was definitely uncomfortable as I remember having trouble sleeping and when I did eventually fall asleep it was only to find myself in a bad dream, where I was 80 something and still going through these same cycles of behaviour. I dismissed it when I woke up, after all it was just a dream.

21st

I'm back now, you Dad had left the lights on for me

I was just wondering how long it would be til you text me lol. That was kind of him, obviously expected you home, you dirty stop out!

Well that happens when you
can't keep your hands off a
beautiful woman

Well I guess you do have good taste.
Going to try and get some sleep,
probably won't work but going
to try.

Are you still way
Awake
I miss cuddling you already x

I managed to doze off, alarm just
gone off. It it's easier you can
bring stuff over whenever you're
ready and we can sort it here?

Ok will see you soon
<Sad face sticker >
Not managed to sneak or cuddle yet
Since I have not had a drink today
I might not snore

That's rather an assumption

<Smile sticker>
I'm only saying

I was pretty certain we were done
and finished and now I'm really not.

It really does surprise me that people, me most definitely included, sometimes only see what they want to see. I saw a chance at saving this marriage, at least I thought so at the time, but honestly it's more likely that I saw a chance at staying in my comfort zone and not having to go through the pain and disappointment of ending my marriage.

I was as well and I decided yacht
I didn't want that and I want you
Let me know when I can come back
Have you said anything to Jack
about me coming back

No just said I'll say good night now
save him knocking later as I might
have an early night.
Why, has he messaged you?

No nothing from him

If we talk upstairs he won't see you

Ok I will sneak in
I will walk over in 10 mins
I have had a great day with you
again today night night my
sweetheart love you loads xxx

I enjoyed yesterday as well.
I slept well and feel really happy
starting this new week x

I think I was asleep within

seconds when I got into bed it felt
a bit strange I didn't think I have
done that since I was about 17
I walked back here with a big smile
on my face I felt like a
love sick teenager

No, I reckon you had that smile
back in 2002. Lol

Yes that's true but I never had to
walk back afterwards

Lol, that's true. 1 night 2gether
and you pretty much never left
and even you had to, you came back

I really don't think you are ever
going to get rid of me xxx

It wasn't until some time later, when I really did want to get rid of him that this comment came back to haunt me, because whilst at the time I guess I thought it kind of sweet, it turned out to have been something of a threat.

22nd

As Abbi busy most of next weekend, this is the last full day to see her for a couple of weeks, so come over when you're ready and we can see what to do today x

Can I tell you something

What??

I love you 😍
Is Abbi ok now

I went in to see her and then she came down for a cuddle. I reassured her she can see you a lot and I've heard nothing since

She was peeking out the window when I was getting in the car
Have I told you I have had a fantastic weekend and that I love you 😘

I think she's probably a bit over tired as well and going back to school can be upsetting.

Well I'm going to bed soon I wish

it was with you I do really love you
loads -

I'm in bed now, watching TV.
Hope you sleep well

I wish I was there with you
I will never stop wanting that

I need any early night
so night night

Night night I have just
got into bed xxx

I'm going to be sleeping soon,
I'm really tired xx

Ok good night my sweetheart
love you x

23rd

Good morning my sweetheart
hope your week continues to be
fantastic as the weekend has
been love you

Thank you, I intend that it will be.

Abbi is singing as she's
getting dressed

I missed you last night
I feel really happy

Let's hope things really
start to finally improve x

It has improved so far and
it's going to get even better
I think she is happy just now
as well
Even you dad is pleased on how
we are getting on
I might have to come and see you
later I don't think I can go to sleep
without giving you a goodnight
hug and kiss

Your fb message might get a few
people asking questions

Don't talk about us yet please,
don't want to jinx things xx

I won't all I saying is that
I'm happy

That's lovely to hear

What's happening between us is
private and will stay that way
until we you me wants anyone
to know x

I thought so but I'm still getting
used to you being happy and
positive stuff so thought you
might get carried away x

The only thing I am going to get
carried away with is kissing and
cuddling you
I don't know if I have told you this
I am in a really happy place and
love you loads xxx
I wish I wasn't working today so
that I could come over and see you
Guess what

This time it had better be that
you've won the lottery!!!

I'm not going to tell you now

Oh well, I will just have to guess

Do you want any of the chinese for dinner?

No thank you I don't know what
I will have yet maybe some chips
after seeing counsellor.

R you home?

I was home for a couple of minutes
but now at your dads

Yes I just wanted to make sure
and to tell you first how I was feeling
Only because I am doing this for me
so that we can be together forever
and have nothing in our way to
hold us me and you back from
getting what we want

That's good. I get that and I
appreciate you're probably
nervous about your first session
but I do appreciate that you are
doing it

I really do mean what I'm saying
and I really want to eventually
put all this behind us

Even if it gets a bit tough
working through stuff?

Just to let you know I am 100%
certain you are my soulmate xxx

Didn't know you believed in them

I believe we are meant to be
together for ever so yes I must I am
just about to go in

Ok, just be honest and open and
I'll see you later

I have just come out

R you ok?

He never replied to this message, so I had no idea whether he was okay or not.

Good night my love sleep well
and I will see you tomorrow xxx

24th

Good morning my darling hope you
have a wonderful day I really love
xxx

Hope you're day is great.
I dreamt you were applying for a
new job last night, let's hope the
future takes us in that direction x

Dad has just invited us to dinner,

so looks like I will be seeing you,
if that's ok?

Ok course it is I was planning in
seeing you later anyway I was
going to walk back with Abbi
when it was her bed time put her
to bed then have a cuddle with you.
Do you know I feel really happy
comfortable and content with you
I have not felt like this with you
for along time love being with you
again and it's brilliant.
And I think I am finally becoming
my true self I'm not a bad person
I think I know this is waffle so I
hope you can read between the
lines on what I'm trying to say
you know i'm not the best with
words sometimes I think I get
there in the end xxx

Sorry didn't reply earlier,
thought client was 10.30 then
realised it was 10, so literally
threw clothes on and ran out house.

I really hope so, I don't think
you're a bad person but you did
become bad for me. Let's
hope we can get to a good place.

That's exactly what I want I with me
being able to recognise it will help us
grow stronger.
I think what I'm trying to say is
I'm happy in my self and feel
confidence in my self just now
at it feels strange and great at the

same time plus I know I have
issues and I'm for the first time
in my life want to resolve them so
can be the person I should be
I don't think I have told you today
so far I love you sweetheart xxx

Wow, there is so much here,
I'm not really sure what to say.

I just wanted you to know how I
feel and share with you if it's ok
xx

Of course, I'm just adjusting
to the new you.

It's like someone has taken away
a grumpy, growling old dog and
given me a young, happy
boisterous puppy lol

You are totally right I have been
a grumpy and horrible person
and know deep down inside me I
am not that type of person and
have finally realised that I have
to find out why I was like that
and get rid of what was is causing
it so I can be the person I am truly
supposed to be xx

Did you discuss this with the
counsellor, or is this what you
have been thinking cos it sounds
a bit like counselling speak?

I have been talking about it to you
and now her.
I'm not saying I'm going to be perfect
I want to be able to control my
anger better.

If you work through things you
won't be so angry. So it is a
really good start. I'm not being
negative, this is quite new for
me 2.

I know it is I just feel I have to
tell it makes me feel better
knowing that you know I'm doing
his for me think I'm waffling a
bit but I'm feeling good at being
able to talk to you able it.

That's ok, talking more helps,
when 2 people are working
together that is xx

His behaviour did seem to have changed and if I didn't know better, I would think that this was a genuine attempt to win me back, to prove that he loved me. But looking back this was not the first time that he had tried to charm me into believing that he had changed. Not the first time he had tried to convince me that I could be secure with him and in our relationship.

I realise that he had learnt how to tell me not only what I wanted to hear, but he did this after he had pushed me to such a low place, that I was really vulnerable and easily convinced that he meant it 'this time.'

I always wanted to see the best in him and hoped that he would really change this time, but every single time, this new and improved version of him never lasted for any length of time. He always reverted to old behaviour and I realised that each time this disappointment happened, I became less trusting of him.

As I said earlier I feel
comfortable and confident
with you more than I have felt for
a long time so now I can honestly
say talk to you about anything
without getting stressed about it
I really really really love you
and want to spend the rest of my
life with you and both of us
being happy.

I hope you really mean it.

Do you want me to get you a bottle
of wine or something else
for tonight?

?

Bacardi

No it's ok thanks, I've got a bit
of a bottle of wine left,
that's enough

u will have to get Abbi to ask me to
come back with you to put her to
bed and make sure your dad hears
it so I can see you later xxx

Oh, I thought you were bringing
her back anyway.

I'm looking forward to seeing
you later xxx
I am really looking forward to
seeing you later

He did come round later on and he continued to be nice, but it was nothing of any real substance. He said how much he loved me, that he meant it this time, that things would be different and that he couldn't imagine his life without me. It wasn't until later that I realised that there were no real plans in place here. He didn't talk about what he was going to do differently, how exactly he was going to change, or what he, or we could do in the future to actually improve our circumstances and relationship.

Good night my love sleep well
love you

Good night. Thank you 4 talking
2 me. Sleep well xx

All I wat is to be able to talk to
you about anything xxx
I am really happy that I can
finally tell you stuff love you
loads xxx

Despite his comments about being able to tell me anything, I don't recall us discussing too much. He periodically told me that he loved me, that he was happy he could talk to me about his feelings, but other than telling me that us being apart made him sad, that he felt he could never be happy without me or the children, he never really told me much.

25th

Hello

<Puppy waving sticker>

Hahahaha

It being the puppy
Anyway good morning my
sweetheart love you loads

<Good morning sticker>

I guessed lol. Just had to rush
and put bin out xx

Just wondering if you ordered
some thing from Lovehoney would
it be here by the weekend

No idea

I was thinking something for you as well.
<Woohoo sticker >
Maybe a new rabbit toy this is
terrible I'm getting twinges
just now thinking about it.
Looking forward to see you later
for cuddles xx
I want you to be the last thing I
see at night and the first thing
I see in the morning

Ok, but that's about you
rather than me...

Ok I want you to be happy and
comfortable with me and not
afraid to tell me anything
My heart is your heart and your
heart is my heart
<Throwing kisses sticker >

Aww. I think we need to start talking about a bit more of the deeper stuff whilst we are in a better place.

Not being negative but I think we need to sort stuff so that if tougher times appear we don't go backwards.

I'm quite happy for you to come backwards into me

Groan

I love you loads
<Love Sticker >
<Heart Sticker>
<Kiss Sticker>

Ok, now it's getting scary

I have changed standing order to £400 just now is that ok

As it's short term and mortgage not due again yet, then yes

Sorry just done sums 20% less should be £460 so will change it to £450 then that also cover the fuel money as well.

To be honest I made it 460 as well,
so 450 is great, thanks

Just changed it to £450 I know I
have that in bank till my wages
go in.

This is another example of how he made it seem as if he is doing me a favour, how he is giving me money, when in reality he is paying me less than we agreed, less than I needed to cover the bills and how he again, just assumed that I would make up any shortfall.

Originally he was paying me around £500 a week to cover his agreed share of the bills, mortgage, food etc, all of which went out of my account. We had agreed to this, although the amount did sometimes varying. We both used to contribute quite fairly, I worked and certainly never expected him to pay for everything, but over the years and especially during these months, there were always reasons and excuses as to why he couldn't give me as much money.

Like so many other times, he always promised to make the money up, but he didn't. What I realised was that he felt I might object less if money dropped in smaller increments, but in reality, the end result was the same, he didn't meet his financial obligations.

Ok, great

I will be approximately £48 less
on my fuel payment

I can't remember what you get,
and I don't have access to your
account any more

£148.5 and £132

Oh, I thought one of them was
over 200

Am I still allowed to keep on tell
you that I love you

Of course, and you don't need my
permission. You are learning to be
yourself, so trust your instincts.

Ok then I love you sweetheart
Did we decide if I am staying on
Saturday night
I just want to have a night with
you and not have to leave
you xxx
<Smiling face sticker >

Remember to go to doctors

Are you done?

In traffic

But you've been to doctors?

Sorry yes

Again, no evidence he went, or even had an appointment.

Sorry I have ordered some food
for everyone can either have it
tonight or tomorrow
I know it's more expensive do you
want to get a bottle of Bacardi
from shop and some dr pepper and
we can have a couple of drinks
tonight xxx
I will pay you it back later

It was quite common that he would offer to get me something, a treat or a little present if you like, but I had to lend him the money to do it. I guess that the truth is, I paid for the vast majority of my own gifts and treats over the years.

Unsurprisingly, he didn't pay me back.

And I have no underwear on
Just to let you know I'm in
bed naked
R u in bed yet
Night night my love
love you lots xxx

Night

Night night
<Panda sticker >

26th

Good morning my sweetheart
<Sent video - Woman say all
the different words for vagina
in Scottish>

Hello

As for the video clip,
err thanks

You might want me to call it any of
that stuff

No you're alright!!

Did you sleep well
How are you feeling this morning
Do you do still want me to pick
up Abbi's sleeping mat

I feel fine. If you have the
chance, will text you
reservation number

Ok sweetheart
I hope that though out the day you
have little smiles to your self when
you think about me and I really
think we have got some sparkle
back in our life's
I wish I was there with you now
Karen I really do love you

This might seem like an absurdity, but in all the years we were together, he probably only called me by my name a handful of times. If he wanted to speak, he just spoke, if I was in another room, he either just started talking or waited until I was in the same room. There were times when I ignored him to begin with, because I just hadn't realised he was talking to me.

I know. Can I ask you a favour?

Yes of course

Thank you, please don't take this the wrong way but I am find all this a bit overwhelming, can you ease off the lovey dovey stuff a bit please

Yes I will

Thank you

Money has been done

Thank you

Am I still allowed to kiss and cuddle you

Yes, but it needs to be a bit more natural rather than constant please.

Ok

Thank you

I understand and I don't want you
to push me away so yes I will not
stop I will slow down

I'm not trying to push you away
and I'm glad you feel comfortable
but you say you've always love me,
it is me that has struggled lately,
so I need time to regain this and
if I feel overwhelmed I'm
concerned I will back off

He did back off, but only for about a day, after that it went back to how he had been, no, that's not true, it became more persistent than before.

That's fine step at a time I will
see you later x

Thank you xx

Thank you for what x

For understanding my perspective
and not being defensive about it

Darling that's fine I know you're
trying to get your head round
lots off stuff and I understand
I'm the same and together we
will get there x
I probably won't be able to get
Abbi because of these stupid
forms I have to filling and send
pictures in they time stamped

so could probably et away with
doing last visit and email about
3 so will leave then

I wish I could say that it was rare for him to promise me something and then break it. He always claimed that he meant it when he said it, but never seemed to care if he failed to do something he had said he would.

Sometimes work was the reason, which I could understand from time to time, but I also know that had he been doing something he wanted, he would have finished his work on time.

It was really quite convenient for him, how often work got in the way of him doing something he didn't want to do in the first place.

27th

I love you

28th

Do you want wine

God no!! Anyway got loads thanks

R u missing my messages

I'm just feeling a bit flat I think

I'm sure it's just been all the
booze and getting up early this
morning
Or it could be you have realised
that you are going to miss not
seeing me so much this week
I know I'm going to miss you

R u still there

Sorry yes I'm here

Wasn't sure you didn't answer

Sorry was talking to Abbi

Ok

Would you be willing to see if
after this week you could make
your appointments with counsellor
a Wednesday?

I can do that if it's to help
you out

Thanks, just cos then I'm free to
work Tuesday and Thursday
evenings and it not
affect brownies.

That's ok you know I will do
what I can to help you out

Thanks, but it's for Abbi really,
but I appreciate the sentiment

Ok I'm going to be now
night night

Ok, sleep well. Abbi will see
you 2mrw

29th

Good morning my sweetheart
hope you have a wonderful day
I'm going to the doctors tonight
to get blood done at 5

Have you applied for a
vanquis card?

Yes and no now that I have cleared
it they are sending me a new one
and I have reduced the limit to 250
and I thought I could use that formy fuel an clear it each
month.

I never believed this, not even for a minute. Given the grief and hassle that had resulted when he failed to pay off all of his previous credit cards, I had absolutely no faith that he would stick to this.

I honestly didn't believe that a credit card company, especially one that he had gone overdrawn on and failed to pay for so long, would just happen to send him a new card. He must have applied for it, knowing full well that he would keep to using it just for fuel and pay it off each month.

I don't think that he ever fully paid off any debt that he ran up.

30th

Good morning my sweetheart
love you

Morning

I love you x

Got a client at 6.30 today now,
so won't be back til nearly 8.

I won't be back till then as well
Do you want me to see if I can
change my appointment
to tomorrow

That's fine, I'm not leaving til
about 4.45, so I can get their
dinner sorted before I go.

I can change it if you want me to.

It's up to you.
She might not have tomorrow
and it's important not to miss it.

I have sent her a text to see if I
can change to tomorrow and keep
it to a Wednesday going forwards.

Ok, if not tonight and just change
next week.

Carole is booked up on Wednesdays
so will Monday be ok for you.
Do you want to go out on Friday

Odd, given that I could count on one hand the number of times he arranged nights out in the previous fifteen or so years. It wasn't just nights out, it was the effort, or perhaps rather the lack of effort that he often showed that stayed with me. It might seem petty but one year I was really upset when he handed me my birthday present, wrapped in the plastic bag it came in. I know it shouldn't matter, it was the thought that counted, but it was the lack of thought that upset me.

That sounds nice

Well all sorted

Ok, where are we going?

Will let you know when I decide. I know where I want to take you after. I'm in bed.

Already? You sure you're ok??

I'm fine just feeling a bit flat.

Why?

Don't really know

Maybe cos you were meant to be going to counselling but it didn't happen?

Don't think that's it but could be I'm fine just don't know what to do with myself. When I feel like this I find it better to just go to bed.

Ok, well just chill out and relax.

Ok love you

Night

May 2019

1st

Good morning my love

Hello, sorry had to leave early
for meeting

Ok might see you later xxx

Do you want to have dinner with
us tonight?

Why don't you come here,
more room and I can cuddle you

Ok, but want to use up quiche
etc if that's ok?

That's fine you bring what
you want.
I will back about 3.30 so come
over when you want

Ok

We can decide what we are going
to do on Friday when you get here x
I have normal wine, Bacardi, vodka

tc for tonight and nibbles
Got some salad stuff as well

Ok, that's good

I'm just leaving work now

Ok

Just go in, so whenever you want

Ok

If you let me know when you leave
I will make sure my hands are clean
and I've brushed my teeth

This was a rather rare occurrence, the man did not have the best personal hygiene. I kid you not, he often had a 'shower in a can', he rarely cleaned his teeth and seemed to have no issue wearing the same clothes for days. He never used to be like it, I mean, he never really took that much care, but at least he used to be clean.

I really do love you and I really
mean it.

Ok, will let you know when I leave x

If you let me know when you leave
I will make sure my hands are
clean and brush my teeth and I
am in bed naked for you
I really do love you

and I really mean it

Did I agree to sex????

No you didn't do a naked cuddle
should be ok xxx

Let's just see what happens x

Ok I won't be in bed waiting on
you I will be on couch xx
I don't know if I have told you this
I have the best sex with you not
quite sure how to say it me and
you have the best sex ever
I wish you were here with
me now xxx
I know I shouldn't keep on saying
it we were meant to be together
forever I know it deep down in my
heart.

I'll be over soon.

Sorry I'm waffling again I just
get carried away.

Yes, I am concerned that you will
hurt me and let me down again.

Darling I can assure you that
will never happen again I promise
I am working on that I want and
will be the person I should be xx

2nd

Good morning my love hope you
have a wonderful day xxx

Hello, do you know that this
time 4 years ago we were
in Edinburgh?

That was a nice weekend
We will make sure we have more
of them

I've just realised that that
means it was 3 years ago that I was
diagnosed and it made me feel a
bit sick

Nothing, no acknowledgement at all, that I was clearly upset about this memory, something he knew triggered me at times.

Looks like Jack isn't going to
Thorpe Park
I'm back

Ok
Left my flipping glasses at home,
only have sunnies

Do I need to bring them to you

Don't worry, I'll cope.

Ok see you soon or I will see you
and you might see me if you
don't get your glasses
You can always feel me

If you want a sandwich when you get here I bought you some nice ham and some roast beef.

Thanks, need to pop home first.

3rd

Good morning my love

Good morning. I definitely like having more space in this house.

Well we might have to start looking for something else

I've just looked up to 350 in St Ives and nothing I like.

I thought there's one in St Ives you sort of liked

Ones I like are all 420 and up.

What are you doing today?

Seeing my sister and at the pub.

Remember you are a married woman.
<More constant references to sex>

Why do I put 'sexual content or references' throughout, rather than include what he actually sent me? It's because I can't bring myself to go into detail about some of the sexual comments he made to me in these messages. The truth is that

I am mortified about it, it makes me feel sick and because I simply can't face it.

Despite the fact that I no longer wanted to have sex with him, that I turned him down so many times and used a various number of excuses to turn him down, he kept pushing and making unwanted advances.

Me turning him down only drove his paranoia that I was having an affair, he just wouldn't accept that I didn't find him attractive and I didn't want to have sex with him.

So what are you doing now x

Just had lunch.

Just got in.

Can you pick Abbi up, just got out the bath and don't want to get wet?

<More sex references from him>
You could have come here for a bath
<More sexual references from him>
You look gorgeous my darling.

Thank you

I really enjoyed your company xx

4th

I really want to see you
So then my wonderful wife how is your day going so far xxx

Pretty good, how about you?

Not bad, what have you done today

With friends and at the pub.

I'm starting to get withdrawal
symptoms from seeing you.
I think I have a serious addiction

Lol

I could try and sneak over to
see you later
I really want to see you

Not a good idea

Ok then I want you to stay with me,
I love you loads sweetheart

I could probably count on three fingers the number of compliments he had paid me over the years, often the best I would get was that I looked 'ok'. Verbal declarations of love were also a real rarity in this marriage and what you might see as asking what I'm up to, is actually all about checking up on me.

I could bring your ipad over if
you want

It's ok thanks

I'm bored

What do you want to do?

Will find something to watch
then bed
I miss you
I really want to see you

I'm sorry but not tonight

I've ordered some blue pills
I have emailed you
I'm going to bed now, love you

Ok, night

5th

Good morning my love I wish I was there
to warm you up xxx
Do you want fillet of beef for
dinner tonight?
Kiss
I missed you
I will bring you a coffee
How are you feeling, is the wall
starting to crumble

A little, but I am still concerned
based on all your
previous behaviour.

There's no need for you to feel
like that I promise
I know why you feel like that
I am changing and I'm not going
back there I'm going forward
for me and most importantly
us to the best life we can have

I love you so much xxx
😘😘😘😘😘😘
I love you sweetheart

This is all a bit overwhelming,
I need you to rein it in a bit please

kiss

Are you missing me yet
I really love you and want us to be
happy for the rest of our
life together xxx

6th

Sorry maybe I just can't change

He had started going on at me about being out somewhere, he didn't like it and wanted to know who I was with and when I would be back.

Ok, well at least we had 2 good
weeks before it ended

Ok bye I will put your Dad's key
through the door

You've ended it this time not me.
I meant what I said about being
together but if you can't change,
what else can I do??

Enjoy your life

Great, thanks

And this is why I don't let my wall down, now I've been hurt again I thought you loved me, was it all a lie??

I'm sorry I really thought we could do this, no it was not a lie

So that is it then, we're done?

As I said I don't think you were giving me a chance. I don't want it to end, I really do love you, I know you have made so much effort in the past.

I can't live with the fear of you threatening to leave every time things go a bit wrong. I'd rather end it now and try to recover rather than live with that over my head.

I know, I just get wound up and I get angry at myself for letting things get to me. Seems like you were dismissing me and not giving me a chance, I don't ever want to be without you.

Then please, if you get upset or annoyed, take time out but don't

threaten me with ending things.
I will not put myself through
this again.

I wish we could run away together
but I've run away before and it
comes back at me.
We could keep going and just
treat this as a little test.
I really do love you and I have
meant everything I have said
to you
I really really really really
love you sweetheart
So can I come and see you
I will understand if you have put
a few bricks back in your wall.

I will speak to you later

We did speak later and it was more of the same, I love you, I will change, I can't imagine my life without you.

The really sad thing is, if he had told me this years before and meant it, I doubt I would even be writing this book.

7th

Good morning my love hope you
have a wonderful day xxx
So what are you doing?

At work, home about 2.
Not going to be home til about
8.50 now

Will you still want food?

No

Ok
Can I see you on Saturday night?

Maybe

Ok I will let you know if I can sort something out
Maybe I can pick you up and we can just go for a couple of drinks and a walk
Do you know anywhere that does cocktails?

Tap room

I don't want to alarm you I had a coughing fit luckily I was sitting on the single bed I woke up on the floor
I think I just go too hot

Are you ok?

I think so
Going to bed now sweetheart love you night night
<Love gif>
<Love gif>
<Love gif>

<Love gif>

I had pretty much given up asking to stop sending so many lovely dovey messages, as he didn't seem to listen.

8th

Good morning my love hope you
have a wonderful day love you

Morning

If I finish work early can I
see you
I might be done by 12.30

Sorry I will be out

Do you want to have dinner with
me tonight?

Ok, that will be nice

Ok speak to you later

Ok. What time do you
want us?

Whenever you want,
I'm just on way to hospital

Ok

They say I've not got an appointment,
got one now it's really bad

What? Who called then?

They think it was the call centre
getting x-ray now

I played them the message

All good on way back now

That's good and ok
Go back 6 months and a good chance they can remove metal work (metal that had been put in his leg after he broke it).

He later claimed that his leg was so bad that it might need to be amputated. There was no evidence of this and nothing was mentioned in any of the medical reports I read.

Wow that is good, I thought it had
to stay in forever

So did I
Just coming past Sainsbury's
10 mins
Good night my sweetheart
hope you sleep well love you

Sorry I had to leave, but you were
getting too pushy and I needed
to have some space.

We have many more years
ahead of us xxx
<Lots more sexual content from him,
very suggestive and pushy>

Night sweetheart hope you
sleep well love you

9th

Have a good day I will see you
later sweetheart love you

Have you phoned up for your
blood test results yet?

Sorry no I will do it today I forgot

There was no evidence that he ever had blood tests.

Sorry was with client when
you called

Is your day going ok?

Busy. Was a bit concerned last
night at dinner, felt you'd sort of
reverted when you started
having a go at Jack when
you promised you wouldn't say
anything. He has been doing his
research about his future
career choices.

I just want him to get a proper job

Ok, but maybe ease off telling
him what to do. A proper job to you
isn't what a job is today.
Technically I don't have a
'proper' job.

He had a very fixed opinion on what other people should do with their lives, especially when it came to jobs and working.

When Jack was younger he wanted, not unlike many other children of his age, to be a YouTuber. But he was insistent that that was stupid and that Jack needed a trade or a career. He was less than ten when he said this, and couldn't grasp that he it was highly likely he would change his mind. But instead of being interested in this, he just totally dismissed it and got annoyed when no one agreed with him.

Ok point taken

10th

Good morning my darling
hope you have a great day
love you sweetheart

Thank you
Just checking on the money you
are meant to be paying into my
account, it keeps changing and I
worry when the mortgage goes
out especially as you keep
changing the amount.

I agreed with you what I will pay
you and will stick to it

Thank you

Just to let you know I really
love you

I know, but please don't start
going OTT again

Ok
I don't want to lose
our sparkle
I just want it to get better

I think you constantly wanting to
see me is too much, when I ask
you to back off, I really do need
you to.

Let's talk over the weekend
about what we are going to
do going forward.
Can I still see you
tomorrow night?

Ok, as it was already planned.

Where are you?

Cambridge

How are you getting back?
When will you be home?
Remember it gets busy
I will get you just after 7
Can't wait to see you tonight
Can I take Abbi out tomorrow?
Do you want me to take you
shopping tomorrow
(for underwear)?

I will see you later

Can't wait to see you
I really want to cuddle you

I've been invited out to lunch

Who with? Where?
Only have a light lunch as we are
out tonight
I know which cocktails you will be
getting tonight
Shall we get a cab back tonight?

Yet more questions, checking up on me, where I was, who I was with and trying to tell me what to do. It may appear subtle, mixed in with other messages, but given that I was an adult, telling me what to eat, checking up on when I would be home, when we weren't living together and reminding me that traffic gets heavy at 'rush hour', seemed unnecessary.

11th

Good morning I had a great time
last night x

The change of mood happened within less than an hour, mostly likely because I hadn't replied to his first message. It was so hard to keep up with his mood changes.

I'm really fed up

We had a good weekend didn't we?

I think so

That's good then

Sad face
I'm sorry for feeling this way
I just don't know why

Talk to your counsellor
about it

I just don't like having to
leave you
I just keep thinking it is
Permanent and I sometimes
think you enjoy it when
I have to leave

I do enjoy time to myself

It just feels like we are just
starting to feel like a family
again then I have to leave and
do it all over again I really
truly love you and I want
you to love me

Trust has to be built again
and when we see each other all
the time, it isn't happening

I'm going to bed now
I can't help how I feel
I just hate myself for allowing this to happen

I can understand why some people reading this might think 'poor man, he is trying', but he wasn't, at least not in any real or long term sense. This pattern of 'poor me' when things weren't going his was all too common and yet he never did anything to try and change the situation.

But it has happened so you need
to focus on moving forwards

cos hating yourself will just
keep you in the past and hurt
the future

The way I feel at the moment I
don't know if I can carry on

I'm not really sure what to say.
You were feeling
positive earlier.

To be honest with you I've not
felt positive for a few days
and I don't know why

What about yesterday?

I enjoyed yesterday

So that's good then

I just think I am never meant
to be happy

Only you can decide to be happy,
or not. I can't make you happy

I am not certain that he ever was truly happy. I know he seemed to be when we were first together but nothing really seemed to bring him joy. Everything was just ok, or fine, nothing was ever good or amazing, although he did throw in a few superbs over the years if I remember correctly.

We went to see John Bishop once, must have been the end of 2015 I think and he laughed out loud. I am not exaggerating when I tell you that this was the first, and only time I ever and I do mean ever heard him laugh out loud.

To be honest with you I'm scared
that no matter what I do I will
end up alone and have nothing

You need to speak to your
counsellor about this

I think I'm just struggling with
you not being able to tell me
you love me and how much
have actually not loved me

I'm sorry but after everything
that has happened, you can't
expect me to just jump straight
back in.

I'm going to stop now before
I get myself even
more depressed
All I'm going to say is you must
have really hated me and I'm
sorry I made you feel that way
I will speak to the doctor and see
if he can give me something
to help me

There is no evidence he ever did this and he certainly never took any tablets.

Maybe it's time to call it a
night and you get some sleep.
Don't run a chance at happiness
by clinging on to the past.

13th

How are you feeling today?

Ok I think

That's good and this is the reason I wanted to talk about/deal with all the old crap before we got intimate again.

Are you busy?
I really want to talk to you
I love you
At counsellors now

14th

How are you doing today?

Tired feeling flat didn't sleep much last night

Not unusual after counselling

What are you doing today?
What time are you leaving?

I took a real risk letting you back into my life, I'm disappointed that because it's tough you're now wanting to walk away.

He had phoned me and was complaining about counselling, how it was hard and it would be easier to just not bother.

I didn't say I was walking
away I am just finding it
hard and don't know what
to do or how to respond

Unfortunately working through
your past can be difficult,
it is up to you whether
you give up or keep going
(to counselling).
Remember to eat today

If I can muster up the energy
I had a sandwich this morning
and nearly threw up so I
don't feel like eating

This is hard but you can either
feel self pity or positive

I think I am being positive
and as I said I have never felt
like this so I am confused and
maybe even scared

I do understand, I know it's hard,
I've been there but it will
get better x

I haven't so it's not natural
for me
I do know what I want to happen in
the long run it's just for some
reason I'm scared it's not going
to happen
Do we both want the same thing

I just want to be happy and

have security

I want the same and I want all that
with you
I don't want anybody else apart
from you

The only reason I am trying is
because I once loved you so much
that I couldn't consider my life
without you

If it helps you that's how
I feel about you
Not loving you again
Can I come and give you
a cuddle

I'm sorry but I think that
would complicate things
just now
I'm going to bed now

15th

Good morning my love

Morning

Have you got any plans for
the weekend?

Nothing planned

Can we go out somewhere?

Maybe
Just going out to lunch

Where?
Are you going alone?

No

I know that I could have given a fuller answer, but I was getting fed up having to explain where I was going, what I was doing and who I was with. I had never given him any reason to doubt me, so I didn't feel the need to explain myself.

Where are we going this evening

I don't mind, where do you fancy?

I fancy going to bed with you

Sorry, no

Assuming you aren't with
someone else

No, I'm not!

Love you 💋

😘

If it puts your mind at rest
Philip is moving (away) in the
next few months

I believe you on what you said if
he's a friend then he's a friend

Good cos that's all he is

Ok done and dusted

It really, really wasn't, as he asked again and again, he even asked on the last night he spent in our house.

I really do love you sweetheart

I like it when you tell me you love me

I know, but please don't keep pushing me

16th

Good morning my love
love you loads

What are you thanking me for??

For you just being my wonderful wife

Why has it taken for me to ask you to leave before you start complimenting me?

I really truly love you sweetheart

I don't feel very well

When are you back?
🩶
Can we have a cuddle tonight

Let me know how you get on at
the doctors

When are you leaving?

He said just a bit stressed blood
pressure a little bit high due
to circumstances it's natural
just got to let it do its course

Again, no evidence he actually went.

It's good that it's nothing
major to worry about .

Can I see you tonight?
Can I stay?

I'm not sure that's a good idea.
You're pushing me and then you
get miserable when you leave.

Weather I stay 1 2 3 4 or 5 nights
it's hard to leave

I know

You know what

That it's hard to leave

You are not the one who has
to leave

I know that, I meant I know it's hard for you to leave.

Ok I will leave tonight when you get in if it helps you

What?? I'm thinking about you and how hard you find it when you have to leave

I know so that's why I will go

I genuinely tried to make this as easy as I could for him. I didn't want him to suffer or be miserable, but I wasn't going to make myself miserable just so he wasn't.

This conversation is getting odd. Can we talk when I get in, not sure if I'm missing something??

All I want is for you to want me to stay
I just want to be with you xxx

17th

Good morning my sweetheart love you 😍
I feel a lot better today

That's good.
Hope you have a good day

I luuuuvvvv yoooooo

Where are you?

I'm out with Amy

What time are you back tonight?

Shall I cook tonight,
if I can see you that is
I want to come home to you
everyday sweetheart
I'm home xxx
I have just paid £75 into
your account

Thanks

Don't want you and the children
to go without I know you won't
just want to give you the money

It sounds like he was being considerate I know, but the money was for a bill he was meant to pay, because although we were no longer together, there were still joint bills that had to be paid, but didn't, so I had to.

Thanks

You are very welcome xxx
There is beer in the fridge outside
if you fancy one

Thanks

<Sex reference>
<Sex reference>
<Sex reference>

18th

Good morning my love

Morning

I've just been thinking
about you
Would you like to go for
cocktails and nibbles then back
to my place for cheese on
toast 😉

Sounds nice, thanks

Ok
Where are you?

I have no idea where all my messages went between 19th May and 13th September 2019, but I can tell you that during these months, he pushed and pushed and pushed to be allowed to move back in. Every time I gave him a prospective date he worked to bring it forward. He would say how much he missed me, how much he missed the children and how much they missed him. He would say that we could only work on resolving things if we lived together. He would go on and on about how lonely he was, how miserable he was at the thought of it being over.

Every time I asked him to back off, he did, for about twenty minutes. He just either didn't understand what I was trying to tell him and trust me, at times I was very blunt, or he just didn't care.

When I did see him, he was mostly on his best behaviour and could be okay company. He didn't seem to have reduced his drinking or his complaining about work, but he appeared to be more considerate, full of compliments and claims of undying love.

That said, I have no doubt in my mind that the lying and manipulation never stopped. He upped his game every time he thought he wasn't winning. He went from nice to nasty in five seconds flat.

June 2019

He went to an anger management class, well he said he did, but he couldn't tell me who ran it, or exactly where it was. But he was not going back, and you know why? Because he didn't beat me, so he wasn't as bad as them.

I really don't know if he didn't see how bad his behaviour was, or if he just didn't care.

July 2019

By this stage, he had been to three one to one counselling sessions and a joint one with me. He walked out of all of them because it was too difficult for him. That's how committed to change he was.

August 2019

I was away in Spain for the whole of August with Abbi. He and Jack did come out for a few nights towards the end of our stay and it was ok. We got on except for when he sulked about going to the beach. He created such an atmosphere that we left

after less than twenty minutes and I didn't go again until after he left.
By the time I got home, he had moved back in and although he tried to go about it in his version of a nice way, he made it clear that he was staying and there wasn't much I could do about it.

September 2019

About a month after he had moved back in, with things pretty much having reverted back to how they were before he left, my son told me that he knew his reaction was one of the reasons I had given in and that he wished he hadn't because then we wouldn't have had to put up with him anymore. He told me he was sorry that he had reacted so badly and that he hadn't spoken to me for a couple of weeks.

I knew I had made a huge mistake attempting to make things right between me and him, because it had led to him moving back and it appeared that once again none of us, well maybe except him, were happy about it.

13th

He came in and almost instantly started to moan about work. Someone had annoyed him because they hadn't listened to what he was saying and he kept calling them names and saying that they didn't know what they were doing.

Do you want a drink

No thank you

I had gone to bed early to get away from him, something that had unfortunately become a very common occurrence.

15th

I love you sweetheart

16th

Good morning my love hope you
have a wonderful day

Thank you

How is your day going

Good, client just left,
waiting for 2 supervisee's to
arrive. Dad ok for November, you
sure you're happy for me to go?
A friend and I wanted to go to
Lanzarote for a week.

As long as you can afford it

I wouldn't have even considered going had I not been able to afford to pay for it myself.

17th

When are you finished

Why?

Just asking

More complaints about work. He seemed to think that one of the supervisors has it in for him. I don't think the fact that he yelled at this man in front of others would have helped things.

18th

Hope you have a wonderful day x

Thank you
Slightly worried that things are going back a bit. Two nights in a row now I have gone to bed because I felt you've huffed at me once to often, or got the hump over something I said, including throwing your dinner in the bin which you always do when you pissed off. I texted you to see if you wanted to go out and yet you have, I feel, huffed sighed and had digs at me since.

He never replied to me, I had no idea what had triggered him this time and the next day it was like nothing had ever happened.

I cannot tell you how many times he threw his dinner in the bin and always because of something one of us had or had not said or done. He never really told us what it was, just got the hump and left the table.

19th

Good morning my love hope you have a wonderful day love you sweetheart xxx
What you doing about 12.30

Either at home, or on way home
from work, why?

I'm in Huntingdon for a meeting
hoping to be finished by 12.30
so would you like to meet up
for a coffee

Sure, where?

Garden Centre

Ok, see you there

25th

Got your tablets

Thank you

30th

Good morning my sweetheart
love you loads, I think we are
going to have a fantastic week xx

Thanks, I hope so

He threw his dinner in the bin
again today.
<Sex reference>

Sorry, but no

October 2019

For the next few weeks nothing of note really happened and so I have skipped ahead.

9th

Good morning my love hope you have a wonderful day love you sweetheart xxx

10th

Morning, where is money you left out for Abbi's trip?

I took it in case I need it

Ok

I thought I had a £10 in my phone when I checked I hadn't so that's why I took it

14th

Would you like any help washing in the bath

Thanks, but no. Happy to have a chat later though.

15th

Good morning my love hope you have a wonderful day love you Just to let you know I have started dreaming about you again xx

Vanquis bank called for you, is everything up to date?

Payment was late

15th

Would you like me to have a bath

If you're asking for the reason
I think you are then sorry but no,
I'm knackered

I'm sure you'll be fine
tomorrow 😉

16th

I really do love you
Do you have more energy today
I love you

I did speak to him during the day, it was nothing of note and a certainly didn't reciprocate his "I love you."

17th

Good morning my lovely
gorgeous wife hope you
have a wonderful day love
you sweetheart

Aww thank you

Is it worth me having a bath
and shave tonight my love

Not sure why you keep asking,
surely you should be showering
or having a bath everyday?

18th

Good morning my love hope you
have a wonderful day
love you sweetheart

20th

Can I borrow £30 til tomorrow

He never returned it, or even offered to return it.

21st

Good mid morning my beautiful
wife hope you have a wonderful
day love you loads

He had lost his job again…

29th

I think it is going to be ok I have
spoken to a few people and I think
I may have a choice on who I can
work for

He didn't, his reputation of being difficult seemed to be taking hold and spreading.

Let me know when I can call you

I'm sorry, I don't feel like
talking at the moment,
I'm going to go out for a walk

This is not my fault

Just to let you know I have a phone
interview booked on Tuesday

Fault is hardly relative the
outcome is still the same

No matter how many times he lost his job, it was still never his fault. It was always the incompetence of others and that people didn't like him because he knew more than they did.

Losing our home is still my worst
fear and you know it, how did you
think I would take this news??

He knew that losing our home was my worst fear and yet he never changed, curbed his spending or got a better paying job.

I am doing everything I can do find
more work

30th

I think I am getting to the bottom of
how this has all come about I will
let you later

By this stage, he had pissed off so many people that he had pretty much been blacklisted by some organisations.

In the nicest way,
will it make any difference?

November 2019

5th

Did you manage to get hold of that bloke?

He is phoning me later
He is running late meeting him at 12.30
Ok

Are you going to make me ask how you got on?

7th

Did you take your passport

Yes

Everything ok?

Sorry just got in I'm fuming will tell you when you get home

Ffs

Not with them

Job or no job?

No job in Peterborough but he wants me to go to Leeds

The reason he didn't get the job in Peterborough is because the organisation who awarded the work to various contractors, had essentially told the owner of the company he was hoping to work for, that they didn't want him working on the contract. In other words, if he took him on, he wouldn't get the contract. At least that is what he told me. I didn't question it too much, I figured he had probably made enough enemies that this could

well be true and when it comes to handing out large contracts, those awarding them held all the cards and if they didn't like something or someone, they could award it elsewhere.
But honestly, for all I know, there was never even a job. He could easily have told me this as a way to prove he was trying to get a job and it wasn't his fault that he couldn't. Or maybe he wanted me to tell him that I didn't want him to go to Leeds?

Are you taking it?

The job never materialised, nor did any of the others that he told me he was certain would.

Will talk to you when you get in

He said we would talk, but because I didn't reply instantly, just a few minutes later he called me and told me that I clearly didn't give a toss so there was no point in talking when he got in. Then he hung up.

I don't know what I'm supposed to have done or what you think I should have done. I'm shocked like you, nothing I can say will change anything and I HAVE supported you a lot over the years so don't throw that at me!!

I genuinely am not the cold and uncaring person I sometimes appear to be in this book. I used to be supportive, sympathetic, disappointed on his behalf, honestly I did, but it had happened so very many times, that I sort of ended up feeling numb about it all for a while, and then I started to feel not only resentful, but downright bloody angry. There was only so much I could give a man whose behaviour and attitude kept causing him to lose his job and like at home, it was never his fault, it was always someone else's.

9th

I was going to Lanzarote the next day with my friend and as it was an early flight I had decided to stay in a hotel near the airport. Not only to make it easier in the morning, but so I could meet up with another friend for dinner.

Just arrived at hotel x

I've just got back from hell

Was it that bad?
Just got back from dinner

Did you enjoy it

It was lovely but I'm stuffed

Going to bed
Night night love you
<Sex reference>
<Sex reference>

10th

Good morning sweetheart
how are you feeling

I'm fine that you, didn't sleep
very well. At the airport now,

just had something to eat and
a long awaited coffee! Xx
Waiting for cases

How was your flight?

Good, had a spare seat between
us and arrived about 30 mins
early xx

That's good so you will be looking
forward to your first cocktail

I've already had a glass of
prosecco and 3 (mini) bottles
of Bacardi lol

<References to my naked body>
<Sex references>

Moaning about children and making out I have it easy, strange really as I had them all to myself for several months earlier this year when he didn't live at home and I was only going to be away for 7 nights.

Is your apartment nice

It's a 3 star so it's basic but
I've got a double bed, I'm
sure it will be fine

I've done over 10,000
Steps today already,
my feet are aching x

You must be pissed going to
the bar that many times

Haha, only had one so
far and had a Pepsi

So no sex on the beach yet

No, not seen cocktail list yet.
Just having dinner and it will
probably be an early night
as I'm knackered.

Ok enjoy

Thanks

Well at least you have got a
big bed to enjoy.

True.

What are you having for dinner
Have a nice evening
Just chilling out tonight
So you out clubbing tonight

No

Why don't you send me a
photo 😉

No. I've told you no before.

Video

Nope

FaceTime

Nope. You know my feelings about this sort of thing, so please stop trying to pressure me.

I don't know why he just wouldn't get this. I had been so very clear on the subject and yet he kept pushing and asking, and he seemed to enjoy me being uncomfortable. I didn't know what it was, but I just didn't trust him to keep images safe and private.

I'm going to bed soon

11th

Have you got any plans for today

Off walking, shopping drinking etc in a bit

So have you had sex yet

???Who the f**k with???
Don't start that again

Are you having a good time
Have you heard from Tesco yet
I had ordered and paid for the shopping before I left.

No not yet

Ok thank you sweetheart
love you

It's cold here
Do you think there's enough room
in your room for my bed as well
then we can sleep together and
use the other room as an office
for you

Why has this thought come about?

Just thinking

Ok, I will think about it.
Can I be honest? Forget the job
issue, but when we decided to
try and stay together you made
effort, but it only lasted a short
while and you stopped as soon
as you moved back in. I don't
want to give you false hope.

This really was a pattern of his, he would promise to change, promise to be nicer, to stop being aggressive, but it never lasted. I don't know if I was stupid, or just an optimist, because I used to believe him. I used to believe that he loved me enough to change, but he didn't, he just was nice when he wanted something, and then nasty again when he either got his way, or realised he wasn't going to.

I know things have drift away and
I don't know why I want to them
to come back I just don't know
how at the moment

Maybe we can try and resolve this,
but I am away at the moment and
I do need a rest from it all.

If we go back we used to watch tv
together no phones just us. Don't
take this the wrong way I know
you are expanding your business
and I will back you all the way

He admitted earlier this year that although he had always claimed he supported me, he never really did and as you will soon see, he never really will.

It just seems to be 24/7 I
understand that things pop into
your head and you have to act on it
but could we maybe try doing that
again even if it's only 1 or 2
nights a week

That's fair enough. I am excited
about it and partly I've been
doing more as you seemed to
have given up trying so I thought
I might as well work instead.

Fair dues maybe I had I think only because there are always interruptions.
<Sex reference>

Sorry, but can we leave this for a while, I'm trying to have dinner?

Ok
No shopping yet
Shopping arrived
Going to bed now

Ok

12th

Good morning my love hope you have a wonderful day love you
😘
<Sex reference>

Please stop

You might think it would be nice to have your husband constantly claim to love you and to make references to sex, but it wasn't, at least not for me and not by this point in our relationship. The main point being that I had asked him to stop and he simply ignored me and carried on regardless.

😘
What you doing now
What you doing for dinner tonight

Eating at the hotel

Is the food any good

Pretty good

I'm bored I think I will be in bed soon

He seemed to spend a fair percentage of his time in bed. He went there when he was feeling ill, feeling sick, fed up, annoyed, angry, didn't want to talk, didn't want to do something and for many other reasons.

He never had the enthusiasm to do anything, not unless he had thought of it, or it involved spending money.

13th

Good morning
How you dinner last night

It was fine, off out for
breakfast soon.

Sounds good Abbi not going to
school I had to sleep with her she
still asleep just now

I will text her later,
give her a hug from me

How is market
Can you get me cigarettes please
I have applied for more jobs
still waiting to here back I have
got 2 other agents looking
as well
Are you feeling relaxed and
chilled out

Well I would like this job issue sorted and a little less of the home life whilst I am away, but yes chilled out.

Enjoy your afternoon cocktails

Won't have them at hotel, they're horrible

Ok enjoy your alcohol afternoon
Have sent you email from doctors report looks good see what you think

This was another report about the leg injury he sustained after falling into a hole at work.

It wasn't urgent, I didn't need to see it whilst I was away, it was just another reason for him to keep contacting me.

I have told Hannah to carry on

He was suing the company he worked for and Hannah was his solicitor.

I will look later

Only told the truth you know I'm anxious about where and how I walk

I know, not doubting you

Ok anyway looks like I may have
an interview tomorrow

That's good

It's in Milton Keynes with the
council same role but less money
Got interview tomorrow at 10
might be able to get a bit
more money

That's good

Just got rates it is a bit
less than I was on but not
too bad

It seems that pretty much every time he lost his job or quit he ended up on less money, or at least that's what he told me. By the time he finally left, he was earning about £6,000 less than he had been ten years earlier.

I know not everything is about money. I know that job satisfaction and security is important. But he was never happy in any job, except one and he never stayed, or got to stay at any job long enough to be secure in his employment.

14th

Good luck today

Just got here

How did it go?

All good hopefully start
on Monday
What are you doing today
What time you home on Sunday

I'm not

Sorry Saturday

Hopefully home by 9 - 9.30

<References to sex>
I have washed your bedding
<Sex reference>
<Sex reference>
<Sex reference>
Can you get me a t-shirt
What are you doing for dinner tonight
<Sex reference>
<Sex reference>
<Sex reference>

No, I told you before

<Sex reference>

He just wouldn't listen to me. I was feeling sexually harassed by my own husband.

It made me feel cheap. It was as if, especially after everything, he thought all he had to do was make some sexual comment and I would run back to him. If he really thought that this behaviour would work, he either did not know me at all, or he just didn't care about how I felt. Trust me, I'm no prude, but I don't care who you are, no means no and if that person doesn't accept it, then there is a major issue.

The truth is, the more he did things like this, the more disgusted I felt.

15th

Good morning my love hope you
have a wonderful day xxx
Good news I start on Monday

Well done

I think Abbi is really
missing you

She is my baby, I have been
messaging her.

Got forms back from x-ray
What are you doing for the rest of
the day

Can you order something for me
from Amazon?

Will need money before

Ok will transfer in a bit

Can you put extra in
Have you transferred it yet
<Sex reference>
<Sex reference>

That's predictable

I'm really looking forward
to seeing you tomorrow
night sweetheart xxx
I think I missed you
<Sex reference>
<Sex reference>
<Sex reference>

<Sex reference>

When telling him no didn't work, I tried simply ignoring his comments.

R u still out

Yep

Ok I'm going to bed soon
<Sex reference>

Ok, sleep well

<Sex reference>

16th

Good morning my love
Did you have a good time
last night
What time do you leave
for airport

Between 12 - 12.20

No cocktails today
So are you looking forward to
coming home
You didn't message me last night

Out enjoying ourselves and
wanted one night off from
constant messages.

So since I'm back at work do you
want to see if we can go away for
new year's

We can definitely look.

I didn't get my hopes up given that I had paid for the last I don't know how many holidays and had had to take over the mortgage and a growing number of bills with ever decreasing help from him.

19th

Good morning my love hope you
have a wonderful day
love you sweetheart
Can you please put £20 in my
account so I can get a
coffee and lunch

Ok

Thank you sweetheart
What time are you home
<Sex reference and sulking
as didn't get what he wanted>

21st

What time will you be home

It's like I was being checked on every day. It was always a variety of where are you, what are you doing, who are you with, when will you be home.

I guess from some people this would be lovely, it might show that they care, but to me it felt like he was trying to monitor my every move. It's not that I kept secrets from him,

I had no issue telling him what I was doing or who I was with as a general rule, but it was getting excessive.

22nd

Good morning my love hope you
havea wonderful day
love you sweetheart
Can you put some money in my
account please as my fuel light
has come on and I don't want to
risk running out

Again? Ok

He earnt more money than me, I don't know why he never had any. This was the second time in three days that he needed money and I know that sometimes he asked for money for fuel or food or something, but he spent it on cigarettes. He knew how I felt about him smoking, especially around me and the children, so he never asked directly for money to buy them, he just lied about what he wanted money for.

I guess some people will be wondering why I didn't just stop giving him money. The truth is, it was easier to give him the money than to deal with the fallout of nasty comments, accusations or him going through my things and taking it anyway. I figured that I gave it to him, although it has to be said, not happily or freely, that at least I had some control, that he wouldn't just take however much he wanted.

Where are you

Out with Amy

Ok

Why do you keep asking where I am?

He didn't answer me. He never answered me when I asked why he kept asking where I was and who I was with.

23rd

I don't feel very well

Sorry, nothing I can do,
as I'm running a course.

I know that this sounds rather cold hearted, but when I was away working, there always seemed to be something and usually it was something I could do nothing about. It was the same when I was with clients, he just didn't seem to grasp that I couldn't just interrupt them in order to read his messages or take his calls.

And by the time I got home later that day, he was absolutely fine and more than a little drunk. He wasn't happy that I had "ignored" his suffering but he ended up, not unusually, going to bed early, so I got to enjoy my evening.

27th

How's your day going today x

Vanquis just called here to
talk to you

I spoke to them at 2.14

Weird cos they phoned here
10 mins ago

Was it a 01041 number

0800

What time are you home

I got told off today for laughing too much. We were watching something on the television and it made me laugh. He didn't like it and I kid you not, he actually had a go at me for laughing too much.

28th

Good morning my love you have a
wonderful day
love you sweetheart
😘

Vanquis have just called again.
Is there a problem, are they
going to start calling every
day again?

A few years previously, he had taken out a credit card with them and then just not paid anything other than sporadic minimum payments and ended up owing them loads of money. They were calling every day, sometimes several times a day. It didn't seem to bother him, he often claimed to have spoken to them and had made some type of repayment plan with them, but given the number of times they called, it seemed doubtful.

He would just ignore the problem and then wait until the debt was sold on, or they told him he could pay off a much lower amount, just so it was cleared and then he would, well usually, he would ask me for the money.

I did give him money for debts a few times, but then I started saying no, which he didn't like, but I had got to the place where it was his debt, in his name and it really wasn't my problem.

No problem it's all sorted

It wasn't!

Can you put some money in my account please as my fuel gauge is not even moving now if you put £40 in

Ok but that does leave me rather short

This was the third time in nine days that he had asked me for money, totaling around £100 and he never returned any of it.

Why didn't I say no, why did I keep enabling him? Well at the time I didn't realise I was. The previous years had taught me that in the long run it was easier to give him the money then to have to try and deal with more aggression and accusations of not caring, or worse.

29th

Good morning my love hope you have a wonderful day love you sweetheart Do you want to go out tonight

Can I let you know later?

Ok

Have you been paid then?

Not yet I have been chasing it
all morning

He wanted to go out, but he hadn't been paid. This meant he would be expecting me to pay.

I told agency that if I don't get
paid today I will not be at work
Monday and they will have to
explain it to the council

This was rather a standard response of his, if they don't do this, then I'm not doing that, that sort of thing, but he never followed through.

Rather cutting off your nose to
spite your face don't you think?
No money today and then a day's
lost pay?

I was only saying that to them

Vanquis bank called again,
this time with an automated
message for you!!

I think the only time the landline rang these days, was people chasing him for money.

December 2019

2nd

Good morning my love hope
you have a wonderful day
love you sweetheart
I have a feeling that this is
going to be a fantastic week
for both of us

I have gone overdrawn because
money wasn't paid in
I've just had my Level 3
counselling course accredited

That great news

He came home and almost immediately started moaning on about work again.

3rd

Good morning my sweetheart hope
you have a fantastic day today
love you

I was quite upset when you came in
last night. I know you had said that it
was good when I texted you, but you
said nothing to me in person.
No proud of you, no hug, no kiss,
nothing. I made a comment you said
yes then started moaning on about
your job.

He had told me twice he was proud of me in the whole time I had known him and on one of those occasions he was drunk.

I did say to you that's good and mentioned about your website to see when you where getting it up and running I thought I was being interested in what you are doing I sorry if I upset you I didn't mean to x

No, you said nothing, until I said do you have a clever wife or what, you said yes. The only other thing you said is the more you have the more you can sell. Nothing about me personally.

Ok sorry

Okay, I guess I sound a bit like a petulant child here, but I had worked really hard and I simply wanted some genuine response, or something really positive from him. I don't know.

He was never interested in my work, he thought hypnotherapy was rubbish, that counselling was stupid and pointless and the only time he did show interest in anything work related was when it came down to how much money I could make.

4th

Good morning my love hope you have a wonderful day

love you sweetheart
When will you be home
Have got Abbi and Jack a
couple of Christmas presents

Ok

Have you checked the bank yet?
I have realised the reason I went
overdrawn is because of money
from your account again.

I delayed it in case I needed it

He owed me money, but instead of paying it to me as promised, he had kept it just in case he needed it, pushing me into being overdrawn.

My life had become a constant choice, either giving him money and risking not having enough, or suffering the consequences of him becoming aggressive, violent even or of him not speaking to me, in order to punish me for not doing what he wanted. He would deliberately overspend on things he wanted, knowing that I would pay any bills that needed to be paid. I did this because the stress of late payments and threatening letters was worse than going a bit short.

6th

Good morning my love hope
you have a wonderful day
love you sweetheart

Still not got the rest of my
money yet

I've covered your share again

Will you be home for
dinner tonight

No apology, no thank you, no 'I'll pay you back', just a change of subject.

7th

How is your day going
Let me know when you are on your
way home
Dinner is sorted
I have had a bath and shave so
desert could be good

Sorry but you knew I was
assessing all day, just leaving

9th

You seemed a bit put out
yesterday when you said that at
least when you were an ass you
apologised, and then well at
least I apologise now?

To be honest I didn't even give it
another thought

I was trying to explain that an
apology, even a sincere one,
doesn't wipe out years of stuff.

Why are you dragging this up?

When Jack got upset yesterday, it bought it back when you used to slam and smash stuff, it just freaked me a little.

What do you think?

<He sent me a photo of Abbi's dinner.>

10th

Good morning my love hope you have a wonderful day

Thank you and you

Still no money, have you chased it

Yes, I've chased it again

Do you know UTR number?
Do you have PAYE ref number?
Do you have account ref number?

I will send them over. I really wish you would take some of this over, it is your money and yet I keep getting all the hassle.

He was self-employed but I did all of his invoices and accounts because he didn't have a clue and despite being promised to be paid for it, I never was, nor was I thanked much if I'm honest.

Fine, will call them later

11th

Good morning my sweetheart
love you loads have a
wonderful day
Dogs kissing gif
I love you
Would you like to snuggle on the
couch with me on Friday with a
glass of wine and watch a
Christmas film

Sure, ok

We didn't. We sat as we usually did, on separate sofas with him drinking 2-3 glasses of wine for every one of mine.

<Dogs kissing gif>
<Cacti hugging>
What you doing

12th

Good morning my love hope
you have a wonderful day

Thanks

Shall I get wine or Bacardi

You might as well get vodka,
cos I'm not drinking think I've
got a water infection and
alcohol doesn't help

I didn't, but I figured he would be more likely to accept me saying no to him without him sulking.

16th

Good morning my love
hope you have a wonderful day
love you

Sorry was in meeting

Have you chased money again?

It was his money. Money he was at least in theory owed due to overpayment of taxes but he claimed he didn't know who to call, what to say, or what to do. I honestly felt sometimes, as if I had three children.

I don't feel well

17th

Hope you are feeling better
today x

I will be fine love you

Good

I might be in bed when you get in

Ok, I ordered your tablets
today. Can you please set up
your account so you can do it?

I had been sorting and collecting his prescriptions for years. He always claimed he didn't know what to do.

I had asked him previously to sort his own out, but he just never did and I guess I just got into the habit of doing it, until I realised that it was his problem and he should sort it out.

Thank you

19th

Good morning my love hope you have a wonderful day love you Do you want to go to the Christmas market

Which one?

York. I don't know of one closer

We never went because yet again he had no money.

20th

So would it be worth me having a grooming session today

This was his less than subtle way of saying he wanted to have sex. I never understood why he didn't just look after himself anyway, why he only ever made any sort of effort if he thought there was something in it for him.

The truth is, that towards the end, not only, as I have said before, not only did I not want to have sex with him, but he disgusted me. His teeth were brown from smoking and rarely cleaning them, he was getting fatter and fatter and he would often smell.

24th

Good morning my sweetheart
happy Christmas Eve I will get
the stuff to take to your
dad's xxx
😘

25th

Not surprisingly, no messages were sent today, as we were all together. He got annoyed when people weren't overjoyed at the presents he bought us. I got more horrible underwear and a pair of slippers in the wrong size. Jack got food he no longer liked and a t-shirt that was both the wrong size and ugly. Whilst Abbi got two tops which she already had and a mug with her name on.

Not being ungrateful here, but if he knew us at all, he could have spent less and got something we would actually like.

I cannot remember what he got, but I know he seemed happy with it, at least as far as I can remember.

26th

Today was pretty much okay, until he got drunk, started getting aggressive and moaning on about having to go back to work.

Luckily for us, he was once again in bed early and the rest of us watched a film together.

27th

Where are you
I take it we are not talking

What do you want me to say???

He had gone through my purse and taken money without asking or even telling me. I knew it was him, because money was missing and I knew my children wouldn't have taken it. When challenged he admited to taking it.

I am getting the impression we
are finished

Not sure what you expect me to say
to that??

I honestly thought I had told u I
used it for fuel so that I could
get this shitty job you just left
didn't say anything if it is over
between us then at least we tried
but this time I'm not leaving
until I get a decent place that I
can have the kids to come and stay

I cannot tell you the number of times he took money from me without my knowledge, often leaving me short and then claiming he thought he had told me.

He also told me, *"I won't go so easily this time."*

Well you didn't and when I got
annoyed, all I heard was
'here we go again'. You often
just leave and I've no idea
where you've gone!
So it's over then??!!

Ok

What do you mean ok?

You said it's over so I said ok

I asked the question but your
quick response clearly shows
it's what you want

No I think it's what you want

He spent years telling me what I wanted, or how I felt without ever really having a clue.

So what do you want???

I want you and us as A family

You know what, I have really
tried, suggested we went out,
spent the last 3 days trying
to hug you , it's you who's
pushed me away

No you I enjoyed what we have
done you something sent wrong
even you to a bit ill and we
decided to wait

That was at the weekend not these
past few days

You got annoyed I was out
Christmas Eve, enjoyed myself
with an old friend for a change,
I was back at the time agreed,
but you've pushed me away,
hugged me with 1 arm and
kissed me for the shortest time
humanly possible

Yes I was annoyed we had Christmas
Eve planned and you were out with a
so called friend that doesn't call to
see you and then again you have to
make the effort but hay sorry it's
your call.

I didn't ruin Christmas Eve
It was spontaneous and fun
and maybe I needed that!

It was one afternoon of spontaneous fun with a friend I hadn't seen in ages and he wouldn't have thought twice about it if it had been him and one of his friends. We were part way through breakfast once, when he left to help someone he knew for half an hour, he came back over 3 hours later and I had no idea where he was.

I know it's been a shit
Christmas I have tried to make it
good but obviously not
good enough

What do you think I've done??
3 Christmas Eve boxes, stuff
for them and you, made stuff,
wrapped for hours

I have never ever stopped you
from going out with your friends
and will never stop you from
having fun
And I didn't wrap anything

That's true but you have made
it hard in the past by trying
to pick a fight, or been arsey

when I've got back!!
I didn't say you didn't just
saying that I did my best,
it wasn't just on your shoulders

I tried to help the past is the past
you need to forget it and move on
I don't think you can and until
you can you me us won't

Last sentence confusing

You bed to forget they past
But you won't

I won't forget the past??

No you won't

I'm pretty certain that I've
forgiven a hell of a lot of stuff
and a fair amount of the past
is still in the present, so I
cannot simply forget it

Ok so what do you want to do
from here
I am trying to do this reasonably
and find out what you want to do

I want you to understand me!
I'm not that fucking complicated,
don't lie, steal, tell me what to do,
ignore what I say and do what
you think I want/need anyway

and tell me that you of fucking
proud of me now and then!

It was easier to have conversations by text because not only did I feel safer to be distant from him when we spoke, but because trying to have a face to face conversation with him was really challenging. He would often sit and stare everywhere else, he would answer with one or two word answers, or simply not respond at all.

He would quite often ask if I wanted dinner, I'd say no, because I didn't, but he wouldn't leave it, he would ask several times, before disappearing into the kitchen and appearing sometime later and handing me a plate of food. He would then get the hump when I said I didn't want it, even though I had already made it clear.

Ok then try and think of it form me
you know I'm not good at
complements and I do appreciate
you and I'm sorry if I don't tell you
Just to so that you know how I feel

I have had to learn to give you
space when you are pissed off
and to not try and overly talk
to you about stuff. I learnt
because that's what works for
you, I don't understand why
it's so hard for you to learn
what I need?

I feel like nothing at the moment
I can't support my family and it
makes me wonder if I can I have
really looked into the easiest way

to commit suicide because you all
would be better off with out me I
have told you this that's why I
have had those dreams

Please don't start this again
it's not fair to me. Earlier this
year you told me you would
kill yourself and it would be my
fault and you hoped I had it on
my conscience!! If you can't
support us, and I'll be honest
things have been hard, then only
you can do something about it,
I can't do more than I do

I know it's been hard I can't do
more than what I'm doing do you
think I want this no I don't I
think you know if I have to work
365 days I would but like you I
get pissed off and need a break
unfortunately I have not had
that chance so yes when the time is
right I may just do something

Do something?

So yes I have failed you failed my
children am failed me I
am worthless
And all this over £2 coins

He had gone through my savings and stolen money from me.

If we're going down this path to

insanity I'm going to stop talking. None of those things make you worthless. Someone's worth is not based on income, it's based on who they are as a person.

No, based on me feeling lied to!

And as I said I thought I told you

I had heard it all before. Every time he took money from me he claimed that he thought he had told me, not asked you may note, but told me. Either that or he said that he had planned to put it back before I noticed. He never did and he just didn't seem to get that my anger was that he went through my things with the deliberate intention of taking, or more accurately, stealing money.

I will come home soon but I do not want to talk about this anymore today and if there is any aggression or any negativity I'm leaving again

I had been hiding out in my office, something I was doing on a more and more regular basis.

I am a waste of space I have tried and failed and failed and failed so what's the point

So you don't want me to come home?

It's your home

Ok, but seriously no threats
towards me or yourself ok?

I have said how I feel

I think after dinner we should just
have our own space this evening?

Ok

I do need to know if it is possibly
over with us or we are going to
get over this

I can't predict the future.

It feels like when we have this sort
of thing we are done it could just
be me being paranoid
Where are you?
When will you be back?

Why does that matter? I'm not
with someone else if that's
what's bothering you!

Ok fine

Tbh I'm just sat in my car about
20 mins away
Just wanted to breathe for a
few mins b4 I head back

Abbi is asking to be honest your
dinner is in the oven I really
give up

She told me later she hadn't asked him_as she had texted me earlier to ask.

I will leave now, be 20 mins at most

Just to let you know I don't think
you trust me and I don't think
you will ever I have tried and I
have failed so I do think there's
anything else I can do

Well I guess that is your choice but
for your information I used to
trust you 100% and with
absolutely everything

It's true, I did, despite evidence suggesting that I shouldn't have, I did.

Exactly used to

That's what you took from that??

No you said it

So what do you want me to do?

Asking nicely

Have a life with out me you
deserve better

What am I supposed to say
to that?

You will never trust me so I
will give you what ever I can

until I can

Sorry not trying to be rude but
is that meant to say until
you can?

Yes

Thank you

30th

I'm home, where are you

31st

Good morning my love
hope you are feeling better xxx

Slept pretty well, just about to
take more tablets so sure I will
be ok. Hope you are on
the mend x

January 2020

2nd

Good morning my love hope
you have a wonderful day
love you sweetheart xxx

Thank you, I will be working,
hope your day is a positive one x

<Cacti hugging>

3rd

Good morning how is your day going x

Got headache but I'm sure it will go. Off out now x

John is here there are going to the pike and eel for a pint if you back in time

Ok just finish my tea then head there
At Pike and Eel in case you are wondering

Not really
Pissed off, no money

8th

R u alone

Not at the moment

<Sex reference >
<Sex reference>

We have spoken about this, please will you stop.

I don't know whether he was feeling put out that his sexual comments weren't having the effect that he wanted, or something else, but later on this day, when we were talking about something we had seen on the television, he told me that I was patronising. I think I was trying to explain something to him and he told me that I liked to make him feel small and stupid by using words that he didn't understand.

On these occasions I tried to explain that I was simply talking in a language I understood, that it wasn't always possible to change the terminology but he never wanted to listen.

It wasn't the first time he had said this. He claimed that when I talked about my work, that I patronised him by using language he didn't understand.

I gave up talking about my work in the end, not that I shared any of the confidential information with him anyway, but I don't think he noticed, he never really knew what I did and he wasn't interested in learning either.

9th

Good morning sweetheart hope
you had a good sleep x

Hello, tbh a bit on and off, kept
waking up and feeling shivery x

Take some tablets

I have and some orange juice

10th

Don't be like that, what the fuck

do you expect, yet more
money worries!!

He lost his job yet again, and yet again it was someone else's fault.

13th

Text message left for you from
recruitment agency.

14th

How is your day going x

I've stopped crying so
that's good

One of my son's friends, who I knew was very unwell and was in hospital. He had spent time at my house with my son and other friends and it was so sad to see him so ill. Myself and a friend took our sons to see him a few days later.

Luckily he fully recovered, but it was so awful to see someone so young suffering.

How is it going sorry don't know
what else to say

16th

I had wanted to do a pole fitness class as it is good for your core and my stomach muscles had been affected by all the injections I needed during chemo, but the class I wanted was full.

Instead I decided to do a burlesque class, because a friend had done several and it really boosted her confidence.

I did speak to him about it, not to ask his permission, but as I was going to be out one night a week, it was only reasonable that I spoke to him. Not that he ever went out, so I didn't think he would object on those grounds. He didn't object at all. I made it clear that I was doing this for me, that it was to help my fitness and to help my confidence, not that I knew exactly what the class involved at this point.

He was fine with it, he didn't raise any objections, or suggest that he wasn't happy, or even worried about me doing it. If my memory serves me correctly, he wasn't even that interested.

I'm not sure he knew what burlesque dancing was, although I found out later that he Googled it, perhaps that's when he decided he didn't like it?

How was your dancing was
it titillating x

It was hard work and sweaty!

Ha just gone to about 10 mins

before you got in did you enjoy it

It pushed me outside my comfort
zone but I'm going back so I
guess I did

That's good so I'm a few weeks are
WE going to get your outfit

I am pretty certain that he never showed any interest in me shopping before now and he certainly never suggested that

WE went shopping for any item of clothing for me, prior to this.

I have to order some stuff this week

Do you not have to go and try it on

No, it's only a corset
Vanquis bank call for you

I
will call them they called me
but was on phone

17th

Good morning hope you have a
wonderful day x

Thank you and you x

Hopefully it will get better got a
puncture at 6.30 and had to change
it in the rain with cars and lorries
passing me miles from a lay bye

I'm sure it will and at least you
know how to change one

I'm working tomorrow was not
going to start weekend work till
next weekend but thought if I do
this weekend that pays for
new tyre

Did you break a glass?

Yes I cleaned it up

Oh, it's just that I've got some
in my foot and I'm bleeding all
over the place

Get someone to look at it
Are you out tonight

Why?

Just asking if you are staying in
was just wondering if you would
like to watch a film or something
with me?

I'm happy to watch a film with you

Ok it's a date I will go and get us
some nibble later

It very much wasn't a date!

24th

I'm walking round Tesco knowing
we need stuff but without a
flipping clue what!!

Chicken potatoes
cold meat bread
Sexy underwear

Don't buy chicken from here will
get rest and you need to give it

a rest with the
underwear comments

His idea of buying underwear had historically involved cheap and nasty items. One Christmas he bought me the vilest brightly coloured knickers, that were so awful, and so not me that not only did I never wear them (not that he got the size right anyway), but they became a long standing joke between me and my friends.

Why he was obsessed with my underwear when he rarely seemed to replace his own, I would never understand.

Are you getting stuff 4 later
or do you want me 2?

I don't know what I want you get
what you want

I thought you said you'd get
nibbles, so you must have had
some vague idea at least?

26th

Good news I think I have managed
to sort out the light issues
with the car fingers crossed

Good

28th

Are you out tonight

No, why?

Wanted to know where you

are going to be

He was back to moaning about work today. I'm not really sure what, I think I had learnt to tune him out.

I now haven't had the full amount of money we agreed on since the start of December now?

I have paid some in now

Ok, thanks

February 2020

3rd

😍

4th

Good morning sexy

5th

Good morning my love hop you have a wonderful day love you sweetheart xxx

Thanks

Have you managed to measure your nipples or do you require some help

No thanks, all done

Have I offended you

No, why?

I sent you a nice message this morning and all I got was thanks no xxx's or anything

Maybe I was just busy? I did try explaining to you yesterday I was having a bit of a challenging time at the moment.

Ok was just checking that I hadn't done something to upset you or anything

Well to be honest I wasn't overly happy that when I told you about what Jack had said you bought Philip up again and made out that was my fault but I can't tell you any more than nothing happened, if you don't believe me there is nothing I can do about it.

He didn't reply, it was like he wanted me to admit that I was hurt or upset, but then he ignored it.

7th

Good morning my love hope you have a wonderful day love you sweetheart

Thank you

How are you feeling today
Should I be naked in bed when you get home

Better, but still crappy.
Sorry, but no

Ok

8th

I will pick you up, where are you?

I had popped out with a friend and I had driven, so he had no need to pick me up. I didn't realise until later on that he was really offering to pick me up so that he could check where I had been.

9th

<Sex references>

Thanks but I have no intention of having sex with you, given how fucking nasty you have been.

He had started to make nasty comments about the burlesque class I was doing and suggesting that I was doing it for someone else's benefit.

I have no idea who these other people were that he thought I was doing these classes for. I had made it clear that I was doing them to help boost my confidence and to be honest, they did. I can't say that the idea of a show and in public made me feel overly comfortable, but that was at least part of the point. To push myself out of my comfort zone and become more comfortable with who I was.

I'm not really convinced that he cared, he just decided that he didn't like it and I was meant to give in and agree.

Sex references

I said no, so please stop.

He honestly seemed to think that he could say or do whatever he wanted without any consideration of how it affected me.

10th

Why have you got a debt collection agency chasing you again?

It's an old one they keeping changing it's the Barclays card I haven't paid it for a while

The atmosphere when he was in the house was very different to when he wasn't. It was almost like a heavy blanket covered us all whilst he was there.

We all got to the point where we started to avoid being in the same room as him because he either sat there in sullen silence or started moaning and complaining. It could be anything, something on the television, the people he had to work with, that he didn't feel well, that he was pissed off, that he had no money.

We are all avoiding him now. Me and the children are each spending more and more time in our own rooms, only coming out for food, or when he has gone.

For me personally, I just didn't want to have to walk on eggshells, or worry that something I said would set him off. I was tired of being accused of having affairs, and of listening to him bemoaning his life without making any effort to improve his situation.

11th

Good morning my love hope
you have a wonderful day
love you sweetheart

Thanks

Can you help me fill in a form

Yes

If he wanted something he switched on "nice" even if he'd been nasty two minutes earlier or had perhaps not spoken to me for days.

12th

How is your day going x

Good, busy. What about you?

Slow x

13th

Good morning sweetheart hope
you have a wonderful day

love you

Thanks, sorry been very busy
and have a really crap headache

I think the stress of living in this situation was really beginning to affect me. I was getting more headaches and just didn't feel myself, but this didn't stop him trying to get me to have sex with him.

If you're heads better is worth
while me having a bath
and shave

Why couldn't he just shower every day like normal people do? Why did his hygiene only count depending on whether I might agree to have sex or not?

Sorry, but no

Ok

14th

How is your head today

8 tablets later it's finally
beginning to subside!

So I might be in luck later

Even the mention of my headache (only) beginning to subside, seemed to suggest to him that his luck was in.

Please know that it upsets me
when you constantly question and

doubt me. I'm happy, I'm getting to be comfortable with who I am after difficult years and I like being out but I always come back don't I??!!

15th

Today was my birthday and having previously checked with him that he didn't have anything planned, I had arranged to meet up with some friends, a couple of whom I hadn't seen for years.

I was going to be staying away, sharing a hotel room in Chelmsford with one of my friends and I was really looking forward to it.

So have you started drinking yet

Had 1 glass of wine and just opened Prosecco as Jane will be here soon

I will admit that I had a great time, I hadn't laughed that much in months and I couldn't remember the last birthday I had really enjoyed. I was with people who knew me as a confident woman and just being with them allowed me to find again, just briefly, that woman that I used to be and you know what, I really loved it.

The other great thing about that night, he didn't text me incessantly asking me where I was, who I was with, or what I was doing.

16th

Good morning how are you feeling

Good thanks, will probably crash later though

You fancy sex later

No

I will put some wine in the fridge

Thanks, but I don't want any

What time are you leaving

About an hour

Ok so you should be home about 2ish

17th

Hello sweetheart how are you today

Feeling a bit flat to be honest

I have pump and jump leads ready

The bullying about the burlesque show was now daily, via message and verbal assaults, it was pretty much unremitting.

On this occasion he didn't message, instead, he kept calling me, or waiting until I got home and then starting. He would call, rant on about not liking what I was doing, but it was my choice, then hang up. Two or three minutes later he would call again, it would be the same thing or he would call me names.

When I got home he might be pleasant to begin with, or he might just ignore me. But either way, once I had relaxed even just a little he would come into a room, make more comments, leave and then come back again.

I take it you've been waiting to
ambush me with that question.
It's different in front of people
you don't know. I am already quite
terrified so didn't want you there
but you wont leave it. So fine,
I won't do it.

And again, another verbal assault.

He would phone me and rant on, saying how he would see me in a different light, or question why I thought it was okay to be half naked in front of other "men" but not him. He would hang up, then phone again a few minutes later, ranting again.

It really didn't seem to matter what I said, it was almost as if he didn't hear me. He wanted to get his point across and he tried to do it in the only way he knew how, aggressively.

He came at me with a verbal assault, saying that if I could do the show in front of others, why couldn't I do it in front of him. I had already explained as fully and calmly as I could, why I wanted to do this and why I didn't want anyone I knew to be there.

Seriously are you
f**king kidding me
???????????????
Why can't you just support me,
this is not like last time at all,
that's all in your head

The last time? His accusations of me having an affair, when there was a real, actual person involved, just not one I had an affair with.

I really don't care anymore

Why, what is it that I've done???
I've never given you any reason to doubt me!!

I had honestly shown this man years and years of loyalty, way beyond what he deserved and in all that time, I had never given him any cause to doubt me.

You do what you want
I've given up

Why, what have I don't
to make you give up????

You just do what you want
to do I really don't care

Why won't you give
me an answer???

Don't have one so
what's the point

You don't have a reason
that you've given up?
I honestly have
done nothing wrong.

Ok it's me then I'm a
waste of space can't do
anything right never can
so you are better off without
me I'm always in the wrong

He would often start saying that he was a waste of space, or a shit person when he was losing an argument. I don't know if he did it to put me on the back foot, or if he genuinely thought that he had done nothing wrong and was saying these things so that he would somehow divert attention and try to make me feel guilty and reassure him.

I never said you were in the
wrong, just that I don't think
I've done anything wrong.

It's done now there's no
going back we tried it's not
working so time to give it up

Are you for real??

Now you might be wondering why I didn't just jump at this, but I knew we would have to share a house and I also knew how he would behave towards me, so I was trying to keep things amicable until such time as he could move out and I needed him to make the decision because then he couldn't get aggressive and blame me. It didn't work though.

Yes I am I don't think it
is going to get better we
tried but I think it was in vain

So what now??
We coexist until money is
sorted out? I assume you won't
try and be a bastard about it?

Yes

Are you absolutely certain
and not just angry cos there's
no going back if we agree
to this now?

I had to check because he often made threats or other really negative comments when he was angry and I wanted to try and make sure he wasn't going to change his mind later on.

I don't think there is anything left for us
I do still love you and probably
always will but I don't think
there's anything between us
you want your own stuff and
you have changed good for you

I know I've changed, I've got
confidence and I think I deserved
that after everything

You just do what you want
you can't even let go of the past
even now you bring it up if you
can't then that's fine we just
have to do what we have to do

What do you mean I can't let go,
you're the one that keeps
bringing up what
happened before!

We are not getting anywhere
best just to except we are over

If that's what you want,
but remember it's your

decision not mined

I felt that I needed to highlight that it was his decision, hoping that this would mean he wouldn't be so aggressive to me, or blame me.

I know it's my decision
I think it's for the next I will
take the blame

I'm not interested in blame
I actually thought you'd be
proud about what I've
achieved and how confidence
I've become, I guess not.

Someone has to get it so
blame me

I'm tired of you having no
faith in me, and actually now
I'm just tired.

I really was, I was exhausted by it all. Living my life in this state of constant anxiety and agitation, worrying about how he was going to behave was so very tiring.

If that is what you think

This was one of his favourite comebacks, 'If that's what you think.' Never any real reason or justification, always put back on me, as if I was imagining things or making them out to be worse than they were.

Can we make it civil at least,
I don't want the same abuse
as before??

I just won't talk to you easy

We can't do that, we still have
things to sort out
Childish but ok
What about children,
what we telling them?

Have a good life

And you, I genuinely hope
you can be happy

Never

Then that's very sad,
and I'm truly sorry you feel
like that

Don't be

We do have children together,
I'm not going to wish you crap
that's for certain

Good bye

Ok

I'm going to delete you from
everything so if you want to
contact me can you do it
through txt message

Drastic but ok

It's only because I don't want to

know what you are doing

I'm not doing anything!!!

Ok but I don't want to know
anything about you from now on

Ok, good luck
So according to you I'm a piece
of trash, but it would have been
ok if I'd let you come to
the show??

He had come into my bedroom, uninvited and started having a go at me for doing the burlesque show, which he topped off by calling me trash. He then walked out.

No I would have preferred you
showed me on your own
but if you want to be
pay per view it's your choice

I showed you the photos, I wanted
to be confident at what I
was learning.

I tell everyone what you do
helping people now I should
just tell them you put on a show
for them

He came back in, again uninvited and likened me to a cheap stripper and walked out again.

How fucking dare you.

What is it £1 a peep

That's why it's over

It's over cos I'm doing a class??
Or cos I didn't show you??

You would rather show everyone else than me that's why

That's bollocks and I've not mastered anything yet so what's to fucking show????

You do what you are happy doing

You have not objected when my confidence has been in your favour.

We have done that before I don't think this is going any where apart from us getting aggressive with each other all I want to is sort out what we need to do

Aggressive, you just called me trash, what's next telling me you hope my cancer comes back again???
I'm done

Do you want me to say that I think you do then it's all me again you said yes we are done

That makes no sense

18th

I think we really need to sit down
and talk

What about, splitting bills??

Everything

I thought you wanted nothing
to do with me anymore

Ok let's do it this way

No, I'm just asking.
I don't know what you mean,
to try and work things out or
end them?

To see how and what we are
going to do

About what, ending it or
staying 2gether?

There was no way we would be staying together, I just needed to know what he wanted to discuss so that I could prepare myself.

I didn't trust him and I wanted to try my best to get everything in writing, or message at least so that he couldn't later claim he had never said anything.

Both can we resolve this or how we
are going to manage it if we can't

Ok, but I promise if you call me
trash again (or anything else)
then there will be nothing
to discuss
We aren't just doing this on
your terms

I think we need to decide if we
want to be with each other not
love or like

I think we need to accept that
things have changed, I've changed
and I think that challenges you.

Maybe I'm struggling with the
way you have changed and as
I said to you last week how I
felt and what I was saying

I'm not going to apologise for
changing, being ill clearly had
more of an affect on me than I
realised. I don't think you
understand everything I went
through, nor would I expect you
to but I'm just having some
fun at the moment, surely you
can't begrudge that!
So exactly what is it you want
from me?

To be honest I really don't know

Then I haven't got a hope in hell
of getting it right have I.

I just think we have drifted
apart and it scares me

Maybe we have but you verbally
attacking me will never help.

When I'm scared I get angry

I get that, but when you are angry
I get scared and don't react well.

You are ok you have everything
I have nothing no one to turn to
I'm to old for this shit and
I'm scared I will do
something stupid

I'm ok because I worked on
being ok, it's taken effort on
my part. Only you can change
this and only you can find
friends and people to talk to.

I always thought you were going
to be the one person I would spend
the rest of my life with

Then it is a shame you didn't
think about that before you
started stealing from me, lying
to me and being abusive.

You have changed and I'm
struggling with that

You will notice how he ignored my comments about his behaviour, behaviour I could prove, and made it all about him instead.

I

know that but I won't change back I'm sorry, this is the most confident I've been and I like it

I'm having an affair again, at least that's what he is accusing me of.

I'm not asking you to change back

Then please decide what you are asking for and let me know.

I'm asking is our marriage worth saving can we move forward

Not unless things change a hell of a lot.

I hoped that if he thought there was a chance, that he wouldn't be so unreasonable, that he might agree to a formal separation, which would allow me to at least escape from him.

I didn't want him, not in the slightest, I just didn't want to have to deal with yet more aggression or threats.

What changes do you want

I'd like you to support me, accept me, not expect me to be your whole life (find some of your own interests and friends), understand that I'm working hard to secure

a good future, stop questioning
and doubting, be happy for me
that I'm happy and most
importantly, NEVER, EVER
abuse me again.

This was nothing new, it was what I had told him before, he never listened then, so I had no reason to believe he would listen this time.

What do you want?

I want us to get on I do trust you I
would also like us to spend some
time with each other I know it's
hard sometimes and I'm tired you
have to remember I get up early
and driving about all day makes
me tired as I said before it's just
the way I felt about what
happened last you and signs
where starting to show it
happening again that was
my thoughts

I'm ok with that, as long as I can
go out without being questioned.
I get that and I hope you get a job
that suits you better.
I understand that but I can't
keep going through this cos of
your thoughts, especially as
I'vc done nothing wrong.

Put your self in my position how
would you feel if I said I was
doing erotic dancing there a show

at the end and I don't want you to
see it but it's ok for other to see it
and also I've been out and had to
peel some birds hand off my arse

He is referring to a comment I made on FB when I was out with friends on my birthday. The man was drunk and I removed his hand, no harm done.

I get it, but you should trust me
and to you it would be about sex,
but for me it's about fitness and
body confidence.
You used to go to strip clubs and
lap dancing clubs when you were
out with your mates, I didn't
question you

It's true, he had been into London with friends several times years before and had been to strip lap dancing clubs. He had stayed away all of these times, and I never questioned him, or accused him of doing anything.

I'm not questioning you I have
never stopped you from going out

If you can't handle this/the new
me, tell me now.

I feel uncomfortable about
it sometimes

I feel uncomfortable about it at
times as well but I can't grow a
successful business all on my
own without pushing myself

into the limelight and
into change!!!

So are you saying if I can't deal
with it then it's not going
to work

I guess that depends, do you
expect me to stop being me.

You be what you want to be

And can you deal with it enough
to cope??

Just have to see
If I can't do it then we will
just have to look at
the alternatives

Like what?

I would assume it would be us
ending it

19th

Am I still in the bad books

Why?

Just the way you left

I said goodbye, I didn't just
leave. I'm not overly happy no,
you were again vicious to me
and I hadn't done anything.

You expect me to get over
it instantly?

Sorry don't know what you mean
and I won't see you til tomorrow

The way you spoke to me!
You really expected me to
kiss you??!

He just wouldn't let the burlesque issue drop. He kept telling me "You do what you want", then telling me I was cheap, that he would start telling people I was a stripper and other nasty comments.

He telephoned me.

I'm at class!
Why did you call??

Didn't mean to
Sorry I know I'm a bit slow I just
realised what you said earlier you
are doing it for charity so
that's no different than any other
performer doing it for money the
only difference is you are
giving it away because you don't
need it I'm sorry I think this is
one sided as I said think about it
in my position it's not all about
sex male and female don't do it
for sex sometimes it's a job

Not sure I fully get what you're
saying, but I think you're saying
no matter what I say or do, you

won't agree with me doing this?

You seemed fine yesterday

Maybe I thought I'd get an
apology but I didn't and you
started on at me again about
the class.

All I am going to say if you want
to do it then do it.

I'm fucking terrified about
doing this, but I won't let
everyone down now and I'm
annoyed you won't see the
benefits for me. But if you don't
agree that's your choice but
don't try and make my life
difficult because of it, you've
done plenty I haven't agreed
with. Enough now though,
I don't need any
more arguments.

It's your choice and your life you
do what you want if you want to
strut around half naked in front
of strangers it's your choice but
don't inspect me to support you
because I won't

He kept telling me I could do what I wanted, but then he kept telling me what to do. He always said he wasn't telling me what to do, but the arguments he caused and the way he spoke to and bullied me, showed that he really was trying to tell me what to do.

Then I guess I'll just have to
live with that, and we'll have to
agree to disagree.

Why didn't I just stop replying to him? Because as awful as it was, if I didn't I knew that the minute I walked through the door he would start and being face to face with him in this sort of mood, was not something I wanted. I hoped that if it was done via message that he would get it out of his system, or get overly annoyed and just go to bed so that I wouldn't have to speak to him in person.

And if I'm being completely honest, I was so damn angry at him that I couldn't just let him say these things without defending myself.

Yes but this not the same
You bought it up about that

About it being ok for you to go see
a stripper, I never objected!
I wear less at the beach but
you know what, you win I won't
do it but I'm still going to
support others and won't
forget this
Like I said you've won,
I'm not talking about
this anymore.

That's about right for you bring
it up later I know you wear less
on the beach that's different you
are not putting on an erotic show
there I was fine with it until you

aid you didn't want me to come
and see you but was happy to let
everyone else's boyfriend or
husband see you ok we will not
talk about it but this time I'm
not expecting the blame
Maybe we should just not talk
for a few days I know you have
changed and I need to see if I
can except it or not

Are you serious, I do one thing
that will be over soon, in front
of people I will never see again
and you say you'll have to see if
you can accept it??
Ok, let's not talk,
I really need some peace.

There was going to be people
there you would probably see

Only women ffs, and
only possibly.
Is this conversation
over now?
Cos I've got a headache

It's up to you know how I feel
about it I think I have said all
I need to say

If it really was up to me, why did he keep going on about it and why did he keep telling me it was my choice, but also going on and on about what he thought and how he felt? It was either my choice or it wasn't.

21st

Would you like to go out tonight?

Can I ask why?

It was just so confusing, one day he was telling me what to do, that he thought I was trash and he would never look at me the same again, and the next he was asking if I wanted to go out.

I just thought it would be nice for us to go out we have not done that for ages

I'm sorry, don't mean to be awkward but I thought you wanted nothing to do with me?

I'm trying to sort things out and I thought this could make a start

Ok

22nd

I was going out tonight with some of the girls from my burlesque class and staying away, in a room shared with two other girls. He clearly wasn't overly happy when I left and commented that he wasn't a babysitter. He was looking after his own daughter and had no plans of his own, so I would hardly call that babysitting. He kept calling me and being abusive, with comments including, "*I hope you and him have a good time*", "*I better not be paying for any of this*", "*I hope you meet someone, get fucked and enjoy it.*"

He would not stop. I told him I wasn't doing anything wrong, that I was away with a group of girls and I asked him to back off, I had to ignore his calls in the end. It wasn't unusual for him to try and spoil a night out by causing an argument, but this was vicious.

23rd

You are hearing what you want to hear. All I am saying is, I can't be your everything, you need your own interests, hobbies, friends, social life etc. I'm not saying we have to live apart, I used that as an example.
You know, I'm tired of this. We'll do whatever you want, end it, don't end it, but make a decision and stick to it.

I m just being like you here something and stick with it no matter what you here one word you don't like then bring it up again and again now I'm doing the same

What, don't understand?

You got stuck on the word trash
so I'm stuck on better
being apart

I got over that, you back tracked and claimed you were talking about those who organise the shows, that and I know I'm not trash.

But if you stuck on us being apart
then I guess I have your answer.

You or I can you stipulated

You said you stuck on us being
apart, so I guess that is what
you want

No you said we where better apart
no me

NO I said we were better when
we spent time apart I DID NOT say
living apart!
Just tell me what the hell
you want?

No you said living apart

No, I said when we were living
apart we spent time apart,
I didn't say it was better living
apart just that when we did we
spent time apart that DOES NOT
have to mean living apart.

You just do what you want I you
want to go out go out if you
want to have an affair
have one I really don't
care anymore

Who said I wanted
an affair????

I'm just say if you want then do so

I am not looking to have
an affair
Are you done with this
marriage or not??

I think so I can't see any way
back we tried and have
not succeeded

Ok, your choice!!

So do you agree

Does it matter, you

have decided.

No don't put it all on me I want
you to agree with me

You want me to agree??
What if I don't, will it make
a difference?

I didn't want it the last time I
was the one that told the brunt of
it I made the effort to try and
sort things out this time if it's
over then I want us to agree
it's over.

Sorry, I don't agree with that,
what effort did you make?

Ok so what do you want to do
from here

Could we just initially agree
to rest this argument and
let things settle for a bit?

Sorry no we need to know
what we are doing so we
have boundaries.

So what do you want?
How are we going to manage it

You tell me

I have already answered
you on this

Told you how I feel I just want
you to tell me how you feel

I have told you

You haven't actually said what
you want apart from you want
me to except that you
have changed

How much clearer could I have been? I had told him time and time again and in detail.

You know what, I literally give
up, I don't care anymore.
I just want to be happy
and loved

I did just want to be happy and loved. I just knew that I would never be happy with him and I didn't want him to love me, not that by this stage I was convinced he actually did.

I do love you I do except you have
changed I maybe don't agree with
everything you are doing don't
ask me what I don't agree with but
this is about us are you happy to
be with me do you want to be
with me

I literally can't care anymore.
I don't know what else to do,
but I can't cope with this or
you anymore.

Ok I think I have it now

If you really love me,
you'd understand me a bit,
I literally cannot cope
anymore.

I think you have gave me
the answer

What, that I'm sat here sobbing
cos this is too much??!!
I wanted you to love me for who I
was not someone you thought I
should be

All I can say is I love you and
can't say I m going to make
you happy

If you love me why are you
putting me through this?

All I want to know is it worth fighting for if not then I'm not going to be a pushover this time I will fight hard

You don't have to fight, you win, I'm giving up, I've no fight left

What od I win

This fight, the right to end this, whatever you want, I don't think I've got anything left to fight with

You are not answering the question it's not about fighting it's about us

I don't know anything anymore All I know is, I feel so awful I can barely breathe

I wasn't this upset about the end of this marriage, but the constant messages, name calling, mood swings and general nastiness. It was all getting way too much and I couldn't escape it or him.

No being negative that's how I have felt all week not even talking tablets help but all I want to know from you is it over cause then I can start to do something about it and then we can sort it out on how we are going to manage it.

The bullying about the class and the show continued to be relentless, he called and cornered me at every opportunity to go on and on at it.

I was so tired and keen to escape from him, that I went upstairs to sit on my bed. He kept knocking and coming in, he went on, then left, came back, went on and on, then left and then he came back again.

"I have a gun in the car, that's how bad I feel about this".

My brain was dancing between fear and 'yeah right', that would mean you would have had to spend money, something you never have.

"Fine, show me"

I just didn't believe him and my compounded belief that he was a liar and manipulator won out.

"Oh no, I'm not getting it as I would take us all out. Wouldn't just leave you and me behind."

As I looked at him in, well I don't know if it was shock or utter disbelief, he said;

"Don't worry, I won't shoot you in your sleep, you'll see it coming and know why."

He claimed he had planned to shoot himself three days earlier, but had seen Abbi looking out of her window and decided not to.

He left my room and I sat there for a few minutes. I honestly think I was in shock and then after checking that my children were safe, I went to my Dad's, even then he was still going on and on at me. Very quickly I decided that I couldn't stay at my house but went back to get my children.

Why didn't I take my children straight away? If I'm honest, I'm really not sure, other than I never thought he would hurt them and I needed to speak to someone I trusted to see if I was overreacting or not.

I told Jack what had happened and he said he would check his car. I had planned to do this, but after he had fallen asleep. As we went to the car, he told us that he had got rid of it. I told Jack to check the bonnet, but it was cold, so he hadn't been anywhere. He then shouted that he had got rid of it days before.

I got Abbi to start packing her things, but Jack didn't want to leave. I was trying to persuade him but he didn't want to go, all the time he was growling at me that I'd better take Jack with me.

I got Abbi in the car, with Jack arguing on the doorstep with him and him yelling at me. I wasn't going without Jack and waited until he got his things. I was sat in my car with Abbi when we heard a banging on glass. As we looked up, he was standing in the kitchen window pretending to run my large kitchen knife backwards and forwards across his wrists.

I told Abbi not to look and hugged her close. Jack finally came out and got on his scooter and we left.

We all arrived at my Dad's just a couple of minutes later and feeling rather shell shocked, we all (except Abbi) talked about what to do. We decided as we were safe, there was no gun and as we didn't really believe he would harm himself (especially given the number of times he had previously threatened), that we would leave it for now and I would call them the next day.

When I told my friend that he had threatened to shoot me, she begged me to call the police, she was so convinced that he might do something to hurt me.

Then the messages started…

21:15 When you phone them make sure it's the armed I will
take every thing I can find and go at them
If I'm going I'm making
worth while

I'm not calling anyone just now
I'm not responding
to any more messages

By then
21:56 I mean it good bye
I wish you luck in the future
22:16 I have asked Jack to be a good big brother and look
after Abbi

He hadn't.

22:26 Just to let you know I have nothing left to live for
Since you not replying you will get these to late
I really did love you
You now have all the evidence you need to get rid off me
Get me committed do want you want I don't care anymore
If not enough will get more

He sent me a photo of every pain killer he could find in the house.

23:04 I totally give up I had enough
Tablets working now

23:12 he called

Ok I take it you don't care
Well fine
I don't feel well just thought
I would let you know
but you don't care
So got some more

He never went out, I had switched 'dropped in' on my Alexa just to keep a check that he was ok. Why did I check in on him? Well the truth is that part of me hoped he would do what he said, and that by listening in that I would know.

23:33 Ok tablets not going to do
so will have to try something else
I am going to succeed this time
I know you don't care
23:59 I know you can see these
I keep on being sick
but every time I'm sick
keep on taking more I will secede

There was no evidence, when I did go back, that he had been sick.

You will now when it's ok to
come back to the house
that's when I stop sending you
messages I have emailed work
to tell them I'm not going back

24th

02:59 Still here sorry talking longer
than expected so will
keep on going till I stop
07:23 I am for now they
must do something at some time
09:19 Are we going to talk
I take it it's no

I went to work the day after this, I had a young client that I was not going to let down and knowing that my children were safe, I refused to let him affect the appointment I had, so I called the police after I was finished.

12:12 I know it's completely
finished between us this time
but we do need to talk about
what we are going to do

25th

I went back early the next morning to check on him. His car was on the drive, but I couldn't get in as his key was in the lock. I was looking in through the kitchen window when he appeared, it made me jump if I'm honest. He glared at me and I left.

He later told me that I looked disappointed when I saw that he was alive. He may well have been right.

A few days later he asked if he could come and talk to me, he told me that the anger had gone now and he wanted to talk. I agreed, so he came over to my Dad's house. I remember standing pretty much as far away from as I could while we talked and you know what, after I had said my piece, he cried, he actually bloody cried. Literally the only time that I had known him, that I had seen him cry, and I felt nothing. I talked and he listened. I didn't even throw everything at him that I could have. I didn't see the point, but I needed him to understand what he had done and how I was feeling.

I remember sort of wandering around the house, I couldn't seem to stay still and he followed me. I was standing in the room my daughter stays in when she visits her grandad, I was looking out the window and he came in the room. I felt like I was both numb and on alert, I didn't trust him, I didn't want to be near him and I wasn't convinced he really believed what I had said.

In the end it got too much and I asked him to leave.

A few weeks later he told me that he realised he had lost me when he talked about the gun.

We didn't much much after this, but the good news was that he got a job and it meant working and staying away. So not only did I get my house back, but I didn't have to see or speak to him on a daily basis anymore, well at least for a while.

March 2020

5th

He sent me a photo of me on our wedding day and said 'Best day of my life'.

11th

He sent me photo of the view from his bedroom window at the hotel

14th

I was unwell and had only moved back from my Dad's house as the issues around Covid had started and he had come back from a holiday.

Let me know when you are awake.

I am

I just looked in and you
were sleeping

I heard the door shut, then Abbi
knocked and woke me up

Truth is I pretended to be asleep so that he didn't speak to me.

Ok what is it you want Abbi to
get you

A cold drink

I think it's clear now that it's
over we will just have to work
something out until I can
move out properly

Fine.
I can't help that you think I'm
having an affair. You reckon if
you have to prove it yourself
that I do, but I can't prove
a negative. Your idea of proof
seems to be me with you, or
at home every weekend.

Fine it's over if you don't want
to be here at weekends that's
fine if you don't want me
here at all that's fine you tell
me what you want and will do
my best to oblige you.

You've overreacted but fine.

No you tell me what you want

I was wanting and willing to
compromise but already have
your life planned out and I think
you have had it for a while.

I don't have my life planned out
at all. Where is the compromise?
You'll seek counselling if I prove
I'm not having an affair by
staying home 24/7?

You go out you stay away it's
up to you.
You just do what will make
you happy.

This seems aggressive to me,
is it meant to be?

Anything I say seems
aggressive to you at the moment
but no it's not meant to be

Then what exactly we we going
to do??

I am leaving tomorrow afternoon
to go back to work be we can talk
when you feel better but
honestly I think talking is
finished and we just have to
short out what we are going to do
until we finalise everything.

Ok

I'm leaving tomorrow about 1
I have booked a hotel

Ok, thanks for letting me know.

Just in case you were sleeping.

In the afternoon?

Yes

Then I'm sure I'll be awake but
I can avoid you if you prefer?

If you can let me know what
your plans are for next weekend
as soon as possible so that I can
decide what I'm doing

Ok, will do. As long as I'm
healthy, I'm sure I can stay
at my Dad's.

It's up to you what you want
to do if you are here you are
here it was more about if you
were going out and staying
out and I may stay away and
work that's all.

Sorry, if I said I was going
away, you'd stay away so I
couldn't go?? Bit confused.

No if you going away I will have

to stay if you are not then I can
either come back or if they want
me to work I can I will work
round what you're doing
I only want to know so that if
needed I can get them to pay
for hotel all I'm going to say
is that I'm not going to come
back just because you are
going away

Oh right, got you. I don't
have specific plans for being
away next weekend so it's
up to you if you come back
or work.

Ok I'm happy to come back
whether you or here or not you
have your own life to live.

Ok, thank you.

If I come back at weekends and
you are here then we will just
have to deal with it but all
I'm going to say is that I'm not
going to come back just because
you are going away.

Sorry again, clarify. If I tell
you I'm going away for the
weekend, you won't come back?

No you might sort something out
to be away for weekend but if I
can't or get asked to stay I will so

you will have to sort out
the children.

Oh that's fair enough. I thought
you were saying that if you knew
I was going away, you'd
deliberately choose to not
come back.

That's why I'm asking you if you
are going to do something let me
know as I could probably stay away
all the time if I need to
He couldn't, this option was simply
not available, he just used it as a
bargaining tool.

Ok will do.
Please don't neglect children
just cos you angry with me.

I'm just trying to be reasonably
I'm not angry with you I'm angry
with myself

Ok

I have now had time to reflect I
except it's over between us I
thought we could possibly
resolve it but it has gone to far
now I will and do still love you
and I know you don't love me
anymore so until we can live
apart permanently we have to
do the best we can.

I'm quite prepared to make the

arrangement as easy as we can.
It's in no ones interest to make
this difficult. I appreciate that
you still love me and I am
really very sorry that I don't feel
the same.

I know you don't feel the same
I'm sure it will ease with me in
time I was only telling how I feel

I found out round about this time, that he had joined a couple of dating agencies, as someone I knew had seen his photo!

At the end of the day we are still
parents we have to do wots best
for them

Exactly

If we can sort it out until I get
what ever I get from accident
then I think we can then go our
separate ways.

Ok

Just ok

I honestly don't know what else
to say. Hopefully you will get

enough to set you up ok.

I thought you might have said yes
we will make it work till then
(only doing what you do to me
expect a response)

Sorry, I thought I had said that
earlier but if not, then yes,
of course we will make it work.

I will do my best to keep this as
civil as I can

Me 2.

And that is why I have decided to
go tomorrow
I feel I need to
Just to let you know the previous
arrangement over the house is
the same regarding my insurance
I will now change it you will be the
beneficiary the house will get paid
off and Abbi and Jack will get
what's left the paperwork will be
here sometime this week and I
will send it back when I can.

Ok thank you. Given their ages it
might be better to leave it to me
so I can administer it. I wouldn't
do them out of anything but it
is of course your choice.

I will leave it up to you but you
only get the house paid off
thoy got the rest.
I think that's fair

I understand that. I'm
not going to rip off my

own children.

And just to let you know I have full
cover from 10/03/2020 for
25 years

He only made about 2 payments and then stopped.

It's your money you must do what
you think is right.

I am it's you that's has to sort it
out I have said what I would like
but since it's over now I will get
a will done just to keep it legal

He never made any effort to do this.

What do you mean it's me that has
to sort it out?
You really don't trust me
do you?

I do trust you all I'm going to do
is make sure it is all legal.

Ok, whatever.

As I said before I'm sorry it's got
to this stage I have excepted it
now so all I want to do is the right
thing so whatever. If you're
not happy with it you tell me
what you want

Actually it's fine. I get the

house, kids get the rest.

And my percentage of the house

So I'd have to sell the house and
give 40% of it to the children and
excess left from the insurance,
so I'd lose house anyway??

No you won't loose the house
they get it if you sell the house

I think if you die before me,
the house becomes mine,
I don't think you can give
any of it away.

I'm only looking out for them if
anything happens to the house
is paid off and you don't have
to worry about mortgage.
Ok I can change it and they get
the insurance if that's what
you want.
Or I can just cancel insurance
then nobody gets anything I
trying to be responsible if you
want it all then have it

What so the house doesn't get
paid off? I'm confused now.
I really appreciate the fact
the house will be paid off.
I don't want 'it all' I'm just
slightly hurt that you seem
to be suggesting I would
not look after kids

You have the house
you have the insurance
you do what you want
with it

This isn't easy for me either, you know. I don't, as you seem to believe, have my future all planned. I'm aware I will be pretty much a single parent and I'm anxious about this and doing best for our children. So of course money will play a role, not saying I like it, especially as money has caused us so much grief, but I have to be realistic.

I would say you can
have my soul
but I don't have one

don't want your soul and of course you do

Everything will be yours and you
do what you see fit with it

Thank you

At this point I was sleeping with my money and our passports under my pillow now, and when I went out they went with me. I needed to know we could escape. This might seem excessive but he was getting more and more unpredictable, the only saving grace was that he was working away.

15th

Do you want me to avoid you
before you go?

No
I'm not happy about doing this
but I think it's for the best. I
don't like seeing Abbi like that
it is easier when she doesn't
see me leave
I feel sick
That was about leaving to go
back to work and how it
affects Abbi

I can understand that. If it
makes you feel better,
she is ok now.

I wasn't sure if you thought I
meant us and that's why you
didn't reply

I didn't reply cos I knew you were
driving and didn't want to
distract you. But you've said
you've accept it so didn't think
that made you feel sick.

It upsets me seeing Abbi
like that
Can you tell Abbi I have just
arrived at hotel and will txt
when I get sorted.

Honestly, I don't think it bothered Abbi as much as he claimed. I have been open with my children and what Abbi told me about seeing him and how she felt never really tallied with what he was saying. It's true she got a bit upset now and then, but most of the time, she barely mentioned him.

Jack, well he kept his thoughts about much of this to himself, other than to make it clear that he didn't want to get involved and that he had no time for his father.

16th

How are you feeling today are
you still isolating

Much better thanks. Will go out
if I need to but no particular
plans at the moment.

Ok just checking

Sorry to bother you can you
ask Abbi if her phone is charged

It's not a bother and she says yes.

Hello just to let you know I have
handed out 2 lots of your leaflets
and card things that's in the
back of the car

Genuinely not sure why he suddenly decided to help promote my business and I didn't even know that he had any of my leaflets.

Oh thanks, that's great.

Don't know if anything will come

from it but if they ask I will give

Thank you

So now you have to stay home
for 14 days

Who does?
No, cos I started isolation b4 the
new rule came in and it was
new cases from that date
Are you ok, you haven't got
any symptoms have you?

Got plenty of symptoms

Well I hope you'll be ok

I will be back Friday

I thought you were staying there
this weekend?

I did to
Is it ok for me to come back

Of course it is, it's still
your house

Only asking
Just in case you might have
forgot can you remember my
tablets please

18th

Can I be honest with you
I have been thinking hard about
this all week
I still love you deeply and I
really do miss you

I'm sorry but I'm not sure what
I'm supposed to say to this.

I'm just telling you how I feel
and if I'm being honest I was
hoping you may be starting to
feel the same way even only if
it was a little bit
I can understand you may not want
to answer me I'm just struggling a
bit to let go of 18 years with you

I can understand that, I honestly
can but unfortunately I cannot
give you the answer you want.

All I wanted to do was tell you
how I feel and I can understand
that you cannot give me the answer
I would like but can you at least at
least think about it

Thank you and yes I will, but
please know the minute you
start pressuring me to give you
an answer I will stop. I'm not
trying to hurt you but I've been
unhappy for so very long that
I'm not prepared to even risk
going back to that place.

I totally understand and will not
pressure you I'm hoping that with
me staying away will help
both of us

Thanks. I will admit I am a
bit concerned about you being
back here so soon, but I
understand there is no
other option

I understand but we will give each
other space
Can I keep texting you though
Just to see what you are doing

I really don't want to feel as if I
am being checked up on

That's ok
Sorry for that

You don't have to be sorry

Ok we will talk if we want to
talk and not f we don't and I
will not take it personally

Ok, thanks

I want to make everything work
between us I don't want us to
not be able to get on

I agree, there's no need
for nastiness

None what so ever

We have to much history and nice
history to be horrible to
each other

I hope you don't mind me saying
what I said
All of it
To be honest with you I would love
for us to sort this out but if not I
want us to get on and be friends
Are you still awake
If you're not then you get this in
the morning I'm saying what I'm
saying because I'm socialising
and I can't bring my self to say I
have split up with you we are
talking about family stuff and
have a life every one saying good
things about it and I don't want
to lower the tone and get people
to say sorry and that stuff I
think you know what I'm trying
to say so it just makes me think
about you even more I have tried
to not say anything to you sorry
once again I'm sorry to tell but
it has bed me really think
about us

19th

He was back from working away, at least for a couple of days.

Sorry for sending you txts
yesterday was just feeling a

bit emotional

That's ok, I was really tired
yesterday and went to
bed early

The truth is, that actually I was avoiding him.

I only wanted to let you know
so again sorry

Another walk with my kids today, we all went out so we could get away from him for a while.

Speaking of avoiding him, this reminds me that me and Jack used to have a system in place where we would warn each other via message if he was in a foul mood, so that we could avoid him or at least be prepared for him.

20th

I'm going to be in 10 mins so
you're safe to come back
I see you have taken our
engagement photo away
I'm sorry I have to come back at
weekends but you don't want me
to then I will try and
find somewhere

I don't leave because of you, yes,
because I painted, I have no
objection to you being here,
I'm not chasing you out by any
means. I am sorry if its hard for
you to be there

I don't want to fall out with you

over this you don't know how
hard it is for me but you just
carry on enjoying your self like
nothing has happened I will
stay out your way I will be
leaving early Monday morning
You can come and sort boys out
Abbi in her room they all pissed
you can clean it up
Jack had a few mates round for
the evening, nothing terrible
had happened.

Will be back soon

I will find somewhere next week so
that I don't have to come but it will
mean I can't help with money
No one but you has an issue
What ever

Ok

I will leave Monday I can bring
Renault back next weekend and
take other one away so then you
will have a car and just let them
repossess that other one

I lost track of how many times he sold my car and bought a new one. It got so bad that sometimes I would forget which car I was looking for in the carpark. On one occasion, he made a deal to swap my car, one that I really liked, with someone who lived in our village. He never told me, he just did it and I had no say.

You obviously want the split more
than me so you win
I have done the figures I can give
you the money for the mortgage
that's it

So what £200 a week?

£1000 a month

Granted this was more than CSA would probably award but this wasn't just about paying towards the children, it was also to cover his share of the bills, at least until things were sorted out.

I can easily go and give you
nothing and you will never
hear from me

Don't threaten me

It was getting more common that he would threaten to disappear and therefore stop providing any financial support. He knew that this worried me, given the situations we had been in before because of him not paying things and running up debts, so it was an other way to try and control me. In other words, he knew that I would be more inclined to let him stay if it was the other option was for him to disappear and contribute nothing.

I'm not I just don't think this is
going to work out

That doesn't mean your children
don't need to be looked after

and paid for

You don't obviously want to see
me if that what you want to do
then I will come back and you
leave to go and enjoy your self
but you will have to come back
late Sunday night when we are
in bed

Whatever, I'm not
answering anymore

Ok you just let me know what
you want to do
I can't leave till Monday as I
can't afford to go and get hotel
so you will have to do or go
where you want
We do have to make some sort of
decision we can't go on like this
and I will try my damndest to stop
loving you

Fine but if you threaten me I
will fight back

Or have feelings for you
Let's just sort this out once and
for all

Ok
I had enough now you can
fight if you want
I don't want to fight you, I just
don't want any grief. Push me
though and I will fight you

Ok I will go tomorrow

Seriously, whatever. I'm done
being threatened and
intimidated by you.
Don't message again,
I'm ignoring you

Will be your lose believe me

Is that a threat??
Seriously are you
threatening me???

Done talking now

I moved my bed as far away from the door as I could. I know it maybe meant it was harder to escape, but at least it would give a few seconds to act if he came in. It was like living with a time bomb, he was just so unpredictable.

Women's Refuge were trying to support me. They had been in touch after the police refered me to them when I had reported his threat to shoot me in February. I had to make sure I only spoke to them when he was out, or I was.

They knew the difficult situation I was in, with him having to stay in the house, and with the Covid restrictions making it harder to go to many places or see people.

I had to complete so many risk assessments that I lost track.

21st

I will be staying at my Dad's
tonight and tomorrow

I am just going to have to except

that you don't love me anymore and
you're never going to love me again
so if I'm being an arse it's because
I'm trying not to love you the
quicker I fall out of love with you
the easier it might become

I understand that I honestly do
but know that I am trying my
best to be friendly, polite and
caring but if you do continue
being an arse and essentially
threatening me over money I
will stop being nice and push
back fucking hard

We need to sort that out

I know, but I'm not prepared for
my kids to suffer and risk
being homeless because you
don't like having to be in the
house with me

You don't like being in the house
with me as well

I have no objection to being in
the house with you. I just get
anxious because I'm worried
about your mood swings and
whether you're going to be
nasty to me

Can I borrow temp gauge
I take it you are going out

Yes, I want some fresh air

Can you do one thing for me I'm
not expecting you to answer
straight away just have a think
first or maybe you can answer it
straight away I want you to tell
me 100% that you don't love me
anymore and will never love
me again
Sorry 1 more thing can you swear
on the children's live that you are
not seeing someone else

I'm sorry but I don't love you
anymore, too much has happened
and I've been put through
too much.
I have told you time and time
again, and I'm not resorting to
childish swearing on
people's lives

I know I have asked you before and
as I said if you are then I know I
will want nothing to do with you
and can move on

I'm sorry but I'm not making up
an affair just to make this easier
for you, because then you
would put all blame on me and
accept no responsibility

Just tell me the truth I'm just
wanting to sort this out if you are

then tell me so I can stop
loving you
I'm not going to blame you

I have told you the truth,
I can't help it if you won't
believe me.

Ok so you don't love me and will
never love me again is that true

I had told him, very clearly, just a few messages earlier (*I'm sorry but I don't love you anymore, too much has happened and I've been put through too much.*)

If it's true that you will never
love me again then we need to
come up with a solution that's
good for us all and that includes
telling the children
Just to let you know my temp
going up slowly and I feel like
I'm coming down with something
I will monitor it

Ok, hopefully it's just plain
old flu

He wasn't getting the reaction he wanted, so he went back to claiming that he was ill. Nothing came of this.

So what are we going to do
And sorry you have still got a
question to answer the one you
will never love me again

I have told you time and time
again, if you push me to give
you an answer then it will
be no, yet you keep pushing.
You tell me what you want to do

I just want to know so that if you
will never love me again then I can
start the process of trying to stop
loving you and if I can stop loving
you then we have got a better and
easier chance of trying to come up
with a resolution and will help me
stop thinking you are seeing
someone else

What I don't get is that you keep
telling me you love me but you
treated me so badly. How can
you claim to have loved me???

All I want to know is have I got to
stop loving you because I still love
you my mind is playing with me
so I think if I have to stop it by
knowing what I have to do
So what are you doing are you
having dinner here staying here
or at your Dad's is he not
in isolation

Staying at Dads, will just keep away
from him as much as possible

So had any more thoughts about
this, so have you got everything
with you

I have my case with me

So are you coming back at all

I don't know

We need to talk about this

What exactly?

How we are going to manage
this situation

Well how do you think we should
handle it?

To start with if it helps I will
say I don't love you anymore
so now we just have to sort out
being in the same place maybe we
should just say hello and goodbye
to each other and not interact to
much but I think we should tell
the children what's going on and
do that together
But first we need to decide on
what we are going to tell them
You don't have to stay at
your dads

Ok, what should we tell them?

Think we should tell them that
our marriage is over but we are

going to live together for now
until I can find somewhere have
you got anything else you want
to say

No, that sounds fine. Tbh I think
they already know, only things
they will worry about are staying
in house and having
enough money

Even my children knew that we had struggled financially and that he rarely had money. They knew that I paid for most things that we did outside of the house, as they had seen me give him money or heard him ask me for money. Jack had even looked at me questioningly at times, especially Christmas day when they found themselves with piles of stuff, none of which they had asked for and often didn't want, knowing that he must have spent a fortune.

That's what we need to sort out

Well based on the figure you
threw at me yesterday we can't
stay as can't afford it

Basically he was claiming that if he had to move out, that he wouldn't be able to afford to give me any money. He could, yet again using this to try and convince me to let him stay.

That's only if we can't get on and
I have to move out

Only reason I'm avoiding you is cos
you keep flipping between I love you

and negative shit.I've felt anxious
enough throughout our marriage
so I'm not putting up with it now.
If you can agree to 'behave' then
I have no issue being there with
you but we need some
ground rules

As I said earlier you don't love
me anymore and I don't think you
will ever again I only wanted you
to tell me so that I can stop loving
you I know that if I have to go now
then everybody's going to lose all
I'm asking for is clarification I
will be as friendly as I can while
I'm staying here but to be honest
when we part forever don't think
I can be friends with you
And yes we can have some ground
rules for both of us

That is of course your choice.
What rules do you have in mind?

Y
ou mentioned it first so
you start

Ok, no abusive, aggressive or
intimidating language or
behaviour, including
when drunk.
Let each other know if we going
out or coming in but only in so far
as it affects the children
No entering the bathroom when
the other in there
No entering bedrooms without

knocking and permission
being given.
Probably others but that's a
start. You?

That's fine I don't drink much
now if I'm getting annoyed I will
go for a drive whilst I'm staying
away just now I don't want to be
left as a baby sitter I will not
ask you again if you are seeing
someone but while we are still
living together if you do meet
someone you will tell me I'm
happy for you to go out

He used to drink every single day. His drinking hadn't stopped, at least not whilst he was still in the house.

You're not a babysitter, you're
a father and I don't go out much,
certainly not for the foreseeable.
Jack sometimes watches Abbi
as well. Yes, if I meet someone
else I will tell you.
If this is agreeable I will come
home now but not telling Dad
yet that I'm not staying just
in case

That's fine but can you please
just clarify that you will never
love me again so I can
move on

How many times did I need to tell him?

I'm very sorry but no I will never
love you again

And by the way I have lost my
wedding ring now the washing
machine has eaten it so that must
be a sign
It miraculously turned up again
and not in the machine.
That's all I wanted you to tell me

I'm sure it will turn up but ok.
So I'm ok to come home?

Yes

Ok, be there soon

I will try and prolong me staying
away for as long as possible
Do you want to try and be civil
this evening watch tv together

Ok and yes that's ok with me

Sorry one more question has any
of this got to do with me not
being able to please you sexually

I hadn't considered that

I'm just trying to find out all
the reasons I know my
behaviour was most it and I
know you have being doing a
lot of diy so was just wondering

if that was part of it as well

What do you mean I've been
doing a lot of DIY?

Have you not being diy

Just wondering why you think
I've been doing it a lot?!
Honestly I think I just got worn
down and tired with all the
aggression, silence, threats
etc etc. I did warn you years
ago that I would one day reach
my limit. I asked and asked
and begged you to change,
you didn't, I reached
my limit.

Sorry having to use your toys for
pleasure because I didn't
satisfy you

It's not really relevant
now is it.

I was only asking if that was part
of all this as well

I don't know, maybe, honestly had
not thought about it!
Can we leave this tonight now
please, it's tiring me out

Maybe not to you but to me it is
Ok

22nd

When will you be back

Not sure

Are you staying out to avoid me

No

I was, but by this stage it was so much easier to lie than admit the truth, which would have led to even more issues.

23rd

He was back at the hotel as he was working away again.

Hotel not doing breakfast or bar

That's a pain, are you doing ok?

What do you mean by doing ok

Not being able to use their services and health wise?

Still a bit stuffy that about it

24th

Hotel closing so I've had to move
Don't know what's going
to happen
Struggling to get food
I'm only trying to pre warn
you what might happen as
discussions are going on

Why didn't I answer him? Partly because he called me and we spoke and partly because I suspected he was just trying to make me feel sorry for him.

26th

We are going to have to
live together
I can't afford to go elsewhere
So are we still carrying on
with what we agreed

Which is what?

Living together until I can
afford to leave and try to get
on with each other

Yes

Ok I have to start telling people
that we have split up just that
I can move on I have found it
hard to say
I still have a cough. Not had
any hot food for days

This sounds bad, unless you knew that he often ate sandwiches, or cheese and crackers rather than hot food.

You are wcloomo to have dinner
with us tomorrow

I don't know where I am staying
next week

Everything is closing

Not ideal but apparently
caravan sites with long term
residents can stay open.
Might be worth checking as
there must be loads where
you are.

That's only for people already
living in them all the others
are closed.

My house had started to calm down, me and my children were spending time together downstairs and I felt so much better not having to see him every day. I didn't want him back in the house.

29th

Happy no anniversary

He had made a comment a few weeks before about booking a hotel for our anniversary. He never did anything about it, not that I expected him too, as he never had in the past.

How much is the mortgage

After all this time, how could he not know, or at least have a reasonable idea of how much it was?

Have I done something wrong
today all I done was peel
potatoes as I noticed they

needed used up

No, I only asked if they were just
for you or for others as well.
That way I know whether I
need to feed them or not

What do you want

Nothing for now thanks,
had sandwich not long ago.
Will eat later if I'm hungry

Ok
I'm going to bed now I was hoping
to talk to you before I went to bed
maybe tomorrow

Was just on my way down,
it's only 8pm. What do you
want to talk about?
Are you just going to ignore
me now?

No I've gone to bed and we can
talk tomorrow

What about?

Stuff

What fucking stuff

I know, I know, I should just have said okay and left it, but why didn't he just tell me he wanted to talk, why didn't he tell me what he needed to talk about. I wanted to know because he had a history of going to bed annoyed, stewing on it all night and then being angry and aggressive the next day.

Doesn't matter it can wait

Then don't bother cos I'm annoyed now that you won't just tell me

I don't know why you are getting annoyed all I said was that I'm going to bed and will talk tomorrow

Because you won't tell me what you want to talk about and I don't want to be ambushed!

Ok if you want to know what I was going to talk about was how I feel

Eighteen years together, he never talked about his feelings and mostly ignored mine, but now, when it was over, he wanted to talk about his feelings all the time? I think he just wanted to try and make me feel bad and feel sorry for him.

About what
So is that why you wanted me to watch tv with you?

Yes because it's the only time we can talk

Do you mean you want to talk about us??

Since all this has happened I
have now come to the conclusion
I don't love you anymore it's
been hard for me to except it but
I now do I feel happy with my
self that if anything was to
happen to me I have sorted
things out for our children

I'm glad you got over it so
quickly and I'm glad it makes
you feel happy

You might think I was being sarcastic, but I wasn't. I thought the sooner he did reach this point and get over it, the sooner we could all move on.

I've had to get over it quickly
just like you I'm only happy
that I've done something to
make sure the children are ok

Good

I know it's going to be a
difficult few months if I have to
be here more can you please tell
me what you want me to do as
in talk to you stay away from you

It made no difference, the times I did ask him to stay away from me. He either messaged me or just found me and started talking at me.

And have you thought about

getting any insurance in case
anything happens to you

Ok, but it might change from
time to time, this is an
unexpected longer stay.
No, I hadn't

Sorry don't understand
what you mean
If you don't want me here
please just tell me

I mean ok I'll tell you but
sometimes I might not want to
speak constantly or at all.
I thought I'd be ok with you
being here at weekends but I
wasn't expecting you to be
back full time so soon.
But we have no choice cos
we can't afford anything else.

I get the impression you
don't want me here if so then I
will go I can't help the situation
that's happening

It's your choice on what
you want

I will do what ever

He wouldn't, I knew he wouldn't. He would often ask me what I wanted, I would tell him then he would either come up with reasons why he couldn't (wouldn't), or simply ignored me and did what he wanted instead.

You can't go anywhere,
as far as I know you have
nowhere to go. Also we simply
can't afford it

If you want me to go I will go I
didn't want to stop loving you
but I have been forced into not
loving you this is not what I
wanted to do but I know you
are not happy with what we are
doing and don't feel comfortable
just now I can only do what I
can do I will stay out your way
and not talk to you if that's
what you want

Again, we can't afford for you
to stay elsewhere so I will be
fine. You must see that it
was a surprise for me, you
back for at least 9 days with
no warning. I know you
couldn't help it and I'm not
blaming you but I'd just got
used to being here with just
3 of us.

You just let me know what
you want

I want to be in a place where we
both have somewhere of our
own to live, where we are both
good financially and where
we are comfortable enough
to talk.

ht, I am uncomfortable,
u didn't want this and
although I know I made the right
decision, it isn't easy, it's not
what I planned for my life and I
don't really know how to move
on at the moment.

And the life insurance, given
that you once told me you used to
plan how to kill me and hide
my body, I don't think I'd feel
very safe knowing you could
profit from my death.

He later denied that he had said this, but it is not something you are going to forget your husband saying. When I went to see a solicitor about getting a divorce, I told her this and she told me I needed to report anything else he said or did to the police.

I understand but just now we have
to live together I find it difficult
to talk to you but I'm trying my
best to get on with you the hardest
thing I had to do was top loving
you but I have and to be honest
with you I have also had to stop
liking you which is even harder
so just now I'm sorry but I'm
only interested in me and the
children and I find that
really strange.

Well I'm sorry if you don't like me,
nothing much I can do if that's

your decision.
I'm only interested in me and
children as well.

However I won't tell you
anything else about how I feel,
as you said you're not interested.
You know what last week I wanted
to cuddle you and hope we could
resolve this now I actually struggle
to look at you I never ever thought
that that would happen between us
and I think it was all because you
said you could never love me again

I am truly sorry but it went on too
long and just got too much for me
to ever to be able to go back. I'm
sad about it and I'm like you
in a way, it's not that I can't
look at you, it's just that when
I do I feel like you're not someone
I know

I think by now I had sort of forgotten how to feel much of anything. I used to be a happy, caring, bubbly woman, but years of this had just eroded it away. I didn't even know who I really was anymore, but I did know that I wasn't happy and wasn't going to put up with being treated so badly any longer.

I'm sorry to so don't take it the
wrong way I'm just being open
and honest with you on how
I'm feeling

I'm not taking it the wrong way,
it's just sad however you look at it.

I don't expect you to carry on loving me but hopefully we will get to a place where we can like each other again.
I guess I'm a bit surprised that it took me a long time to stop loving you but you seem to have gotten over it in about a month. Still I'd rather that than you hurting so I'm glad that stopping loving me helped you

I was surprised, given how much he claimed to love me, and it's not that I wanted him to love me, given what had happened I had started to doubt if he ever really had, but it was playing with my mind, 'I love you', 'I can't imagine my life without you', 'I'm over you' all in the space of a day.

Sorry as I said I have been forced to stop loving you don't get me wrong I have wanted to give you a cuddle and a kiss and have sex with you but I have had to except that you don't want me again so I have had to let it go and had to cut all emotions off and believe me it's hard
And just to let you know I will never ever love anybody like I loved you plus I don't want to go through this again

Ok, I understand that. I hope you do find someone at some point but that is up to you. I'm going to sleep now

30th

Let me know what you want to
do today if you want to talk we
can talk if you want me to stay
out your way I will just let me
know what you want

Ok. When you say talk do you
mean about something
specific or just in general?

Just in general or if there's
anything specific you want to
talk about

Ok, I will try to keep it as
normal as possible it's just
weird that I don't hug someone
I used to hug so I sort of
feel I have to avoid you

I never ever wanted to stop
loving you unfortunately if
that's what I have to do to get
over this then we will both
have to deal with it again I'm
sorry it's come to this I love
lying in bed cuddling you
Just so you know I could easily
love you again

I can't stop you loving me or not
loving me but we can't go
backwards unfortunately
because too much has
happened and although I'm
not going to drag it all up,

too much pain, damage and
distrust has been caused

Looking back and if I am completely honest, I think I started to fall out of love with him more than ten years ago. I did try to love him again, but he let me down so many times that I just stopped. If I hadn't been so scared of the financial situation and what leaving could potentially result in, I would have told him sooner. I wish I had been brave enough to end it so many years earlier.

That's fine and as I said I feel
like I have been forced to stop
loving you and the only way I can
move on is to not love
you anymore

Ok, I understand that.
It's probably just cos this
lockdown has come at a
really bad time

I'm only trying to be open
and honest with you

The irony! 'I'm only trying to be open and honest with you.' After 18 years of lying he now claimed he was trying to be honest with me. I am sure you can understand why I didn't believe a word of it.

I have really wanted to give you a
cuddle but I have managed to
control my self it's been so hard

It's really frustrating that

now you are being open and honest
and you weren't when it could
have made a real difference

Like yesterday I really wanted
a cuddle from you as I was
really scared with the pain I
was in luckily it was just an
upset stomach but I was scared

Never had I heard the word scared come out of his mouth, not once, and yet now, he was claiming a stomach pain scared him. I'm not callous, but firstly he never told me he was in pain and secondly, I'd spent years hearing him claiming to be ill, usually when he was trying to manipulate me, he'd never asked for a cuddle when he was in pain before and I doubted he was even ill.

If you want a cuddle at any time
I'm happy to give you one

Thank you but I won't

So I take it if we can't have a hug
or cuddle from time to time then
sex every now and again is out
the question

Yes I'm afraid it absolutely is

Ok just wanted to check

'I don't love you', 'I don't want to be with you', 'you have been abusive', 'you have threatened to shoot me', 'you have scared me', and yet he seemed surprised that I didn't want a cuddle from him?

I think I need to stop talking to
you for a bit and also try to not
see as you I'm starting to get
feelings for you again

Ok fair enough,
I will try to avoid you

I think I need to go back to not
liking you again sorry
My emotions are up and down
just now part of me wants to be
friends with you but then I start
getting feelings for you its
very confusing

Ok, well do what you
need to do, it's fine.

I'm not being horrible with
this I'm just feeling confused

It's fine

And it was genuinely fine. I was at a point where him ignoring me and staying away from me was a much better way for me to live.

31st

Heard from others and they
haven't' been paid either
Mortgage holiday sorted
Car loan holiday sorted as well
I've still not been paid
I have spent most of morning

sorting out what I can. I know I'm
behind but you'll just have to
pay the difference
Most of these messages came in
whilst I was working, so I didn't
see them to begin with.
When are you back

By 5, why?

I wanted to know
You can as far as I'm
concerned go to hell

I have no idea what I am supposed to have done this time. Perhaps I didn't commiserate with him about his job issue, truth is I couldn't, I didn't care. So many storms in tea cup with him, so much life is so terrible with him, so much poor me, that I knew I would make my finances work, and I just didn't care any longer.

I'm glad I have finally made
you happy

You think being threatened

by you is fun?

You said you are happy now
I'm glad for you

When did I say that?

When you were down here you said
finally I'm happy

Sorry I don't remember that.
You were being nasty again,
so sorry if I don't remember
everything. Why is your
first instinct to attack?

He was angry that I hadn't told him it would all be alright, that we would work it out somehow. I'm not sure why he thought I would do either of these things, we were over, did he not understand that?

I'm concerned about not being
paid I have one everything I can
I you anymore you have done
nearly everything you have
asked me to do you don't like
and I definitely don't like you
anymore you just carry on
being happy you deserve it
after all the shit I have put you
through yes it's all my fault so
just do what you want

He had done nearly everything I had asked him to? I think it's clear from the texts that he rarely, if ever did what I asked him to!

I get you are concerned, so am I but
the difference is, I don't
attack you. I am holding back
a whole heap of emotion to try and
make this process easier so don't
think you're the only one
suffering here

So was I but I know now I don't love
you or ever will and yes I don't even

want to be friends with you when
this is all over so as far as any
emotions nothing now I just want
this over and done with

I want it over and done with but
don't threaten me please,
it won't help

I'm not threatening in just telling
you the truth and yes I don't
believe you that you were not
seeing someone else

So what was 'you won't be
laughing at the end of this'
if not a threat.

He had made a comment the night before, when I had apparently claimed I was happy now, that I wouldn't be laughing at the end of this.

I can't help what you believe,
don't you think if I had
someone else I would leave
here and go there??!!!

Back to more accusations of me having an affair.

You could be doing it anywhere
and at anytime and yes you
might not be laughing at the end
of this and that's not a threat

What is it then? Do you think I'm
laughing now? I know I haven't

and am not doing anything
wrong. We are over and if or
when I decide to meet someone
else that will be up to me.

Good and I hope he or them
satisfy you
I really wish I had never met you
As far as I'm concerned
you are dead to me

I pushed my unit up against my bedroom door tonight, I just didn't feel safe.

April 2020

4th

I have only been paid £1600 so
have put £900 in your account

Thank you

I know it's not much but I still
have my bills and need money
for work
You will have to sort out
payment holidays
I going out to supermarket do
you want anything

I'm confused, yesterday I was
dead to you, now you're
asking me if I need anything?

As in our relationship and
stuff for family

Sorry that makes no sense

Our relationship is dead and
maybe I should have said to I
need to get anything for the
family and not you

Ok, thank you for the
clarification but please
remember that whether
you like it or not, I am still
the mother of your children and
my welfare counts as I need to
care for them

Are the crisps you bought
yesterday just for you
Do you want to eat with
us tonight

I hadn't thought about it tbh and
you've never asked before.
I am confused though, why do you
want me to eat with you if
you wish you'd never met me?

I'm sorry not eating with me
but I'm happy to cook your
dinner as you said I have to
look after your welfare

Oh ok, then thanks but I
will sort my own out

Fine

You ok if I eat in the lounge?

Yes if you want
So have you bought any
new toys?

Sorry I shouldn't ask
personal questions

Thank you and no,
you shouldn't

2nd

Do you want curry tonight?

Sure, thanks

3rd

Would you like a bacon roll?

Ok

It was beginning to feel as if I was living in some weird twilight zone...

Ok you might think I'm being
a moron but I'm not paying for you
to have sex in my house while I'm
still paying for it you will have
to come up with something
to compromise
If you want to pay half the
mortgage then do whatever you
want in the house I'm only
paying for the children to
be there
This is after I move out
I want to compromise as much as
I can but you have to as well
It's up to you how you want
to continue
And ignoring me won't help

These messages came from out the blue, we had not discussed anything like this, he just started messaging me.

I'm sorry but what exactly do you want me to say. You cannot dictate who stays here once you have gone and no judge would agree that you get to charge me an amount per night if someone stays

I have been open and honest with you regarding this I am willing to compromise with you if something you don't like or won't agree with then maybe we need to do it through a lawyer then we can all lose out

So basically I agree to what you want or we have to waste money on a solicitor?

If we do go down that root then nobody wins and as I said I'm not paying for someone else to live at my house

His house? The house that we had bought with a loan from my parents, that I paid more than my fair share towards, that I had decorated, paid for more than 90% of the furnishings of and nearly lost because he didn't pay the mortgage for?

It's only you that can change this you are holding the cards it's your choice how this works out

I'm not asking you to pay for

someone to live here, but you
cannot charge me if a man,
who I don't yet have, stays
here sometimes. No court
would uphold that.

You need to decide how you
want to play it

What exactly do you mean?

It's your choice on how we are
going to do this
We either agree to this mutually
or we don't

Where's the mutual agreement.
You want me to pay you £28
every time a man, who doesn't
exist stays in this house???

Either that or you go to a hotel
or his place
I can just say we go to lawyers and
you buy me out of house then you
can do what you want but I'm not
wanting to do that as I have said
I want my children to benefit
from this

I am not discussing this
anymore, this is just more
bullying from you.
You cannot make me sell this
house, the law doesn't work
that way

I wasn't 100% certain this was the case, but a solicitor had told me that it was unlikely I would be made to sell it whilst my children were still under eighteen or in full time education.

It's up to you
I have tried to be compromising
I have raise my concerns so it's
totally up to you with what
happens now

You think I don't know what's
going on. You are so certain I am
seeing someone you are
pushing this hoping I will
slip up and admit it.
This is not a compromise, this
is you dictating how I live and
it is not acceptable.

No it's not how we proceed is
up to you

I am not agreeing to this
on principal

Fine
As I said it's up to you on how
we proceed from here

This is attempted blackmail
and I am not agreeing to it

No it's not all I'm saying is it is
up to you on what we are
going to do I am not
blackmailing you in to

anything I'm only asking you
to compromise

This is not a compromise,
this is you trying to
manipulate me. You cannot
charge me IF I get a new partner
and he stays here on occasion

All I'm saying is it's
your choice

Are you going to charge me less if
someone stays but we don't
have sex?
What if they visit during the
day, and they don't stay,
can we have sex then????

I know this wasn't a funny situation to be in, but I will admit that I did find it bemusing and later on I did laugh about the ridiculousness of it.

If and when you move someone else
in I will stop paying mortgage
whether they having sex with you
or not

This is not about moving someone
else in, that will be covered in
the agreement, this is about an
occasional overnight visitor

You can have sex with or what or
when ever you want all I'm saying
is I don't want you doing it with

my children in the house unless
they are staying with
you permanently

He genuinely seemed obsessed with the idea that I was having sex with someone else.

Ok let's ask the children what
they think about this
Ok let's just go to see lawyer's
I was willing to give up
everything this way it will be
hard for everyone all you do was
say I will consider it and see
what happens but no

Consider what, that if in the
future at some point I get a new
partner that you think it
acceptable for you to charge me
£28 for every night they
might stay????

You do what you want I don't think
we are going to agree with
anything so best we just get in
touch with a lawyer and if it comes
to being horrible with each other I
will bring Philip in to it from
last year
So it's all on you from now
And yes it's all my fault I won't
deny that but you have had a part
in this as well
So you are probably going to
ignore me now but it's your choice
on whether we do this
amicably or not

I've been being polite and
amicable. You are the one
trying to dictate what
I do and who I see

It's your choice on what
happens next

Stop fucking saying that. You are
essentially saying that if I don't
agree to your terms you
will make my life hell.
In fact you know what, go
consult a solicitor and see what
they say when you tell them
what you are trying to make
me agree to.

Get me removed from the
house let me stay
it's all up to you

Ok I will
If you carry on I will take out a
non molestation order
against you

You do what you feel best

Do not message me again

I won't text you again after this
it looks like we are going to
have to go to court to settle this
and yes I will admit to all my
indiscretions I hope you will to

I didn't have any indiscretions to admit to.

I went out on another walk, I just needed to get away from him. I also called Philip and told him what had happened. Philip is a real person but he is a friend nothing more, we were friends then and we are friends now. Had Philip had been a woman, then he would not have thought twice about it.

4th

Ok you win you can move your
boyfriend or lovers in when I leave
but I would like to get all the rest
sorted out and on some sort of
legal agreement

For the last and final time,
I DO NOT have a boyfriend
waiting to move in!!

Fine, you send me what you
think is fair and I will read it
You said last night there was
something we could fill out

There is but we need to sort a
financial agreement. I will go
through and give you the figures
I have worked it out to be

Just so you know I'm only earning
£860 a week before tax
So take home is 620
I am happy to pay mortgage and
560 a month child support I will

get your car back here but
the other will have to go
While I'm staying here i can give
a bit more but once I move out
we will have to re negotiate

I am going to seek legal advice
before we make a
financial agreement

Ok just remember I can't pay
what I don't have

I understand that

Just so you know when you get your
legal advice my salary is £45000

Yes I know. You need to provide
proof, not that I don't believe
you but if we have to involve
courts they will want evidence.

It might even go down once I
move out I will get you a copy
of my contract

There are certain rules about
child and spousal support you
can't just change it. And before
you say it, the law says you
can't just not pay, even if
you have no job.

I had no idea of whether I would get spousal support or not, I just wanted him to know that he couldn't just make the rules up himself.

I have looked at child maintenance
on government website and
they say it's £560 for both of them
and if I pay mortgage £862
that's £1422 and if I get a full month
pay will leave me about £900
to get a place and live

He made this offer, I didn't ask him.

So have I and it's 586.98 a month.
I get that but also consider I am
still paying off debts you caused
and things for you.

Yes I know I was probably being rather childish, but after the messages from yesterday about my non-existent partner and the threats, I wasn't feeling in a particularly co-operative mood.

What about your settlement?

We will have to see if i even get
a settlement
And fine let's just see
what happens

I understand that but I want
something written into any
agreement. Obviously it will
only apply if you get a
settlement we are not waiting
until then for you to
move out.

I didn't trust him not to lie and he had threatened before to quit working so he had to pay me nothing for the children.

He had offered to share some of the money because he knew that I had helped him with getting paperwork sorted, emailing his solicitor etc. and his solicitor told me that part of the settlement was calculated by how much physical help I had had to give him, so I wasn't expecting money for nothing. Had she not said this, I wouldn't have even thought about this.

If we can sort the financial stuff, we could be divorced by September.

Ok I will move out at the end of the month when I get paid so I can get somewhere
So you win again

How exactly do I win?

And you can be the one to tell Abbi you want me out the house
Your getting rid of me

I'm ok with that. You let me go years ago so don't get on your pity horse.

I'm not so when will you let me know what you want and then I will see what I can pay you I will bring your car back next week and take other away

Ok but you need to make sure car is clean and safe to drive because your children will be going in it.

It will be what it is

Sorry not accepting that

This wasn't me trying to hold onto the car I had, it was about me taking Abbi out quite a lot and I wasn't prepared to risk her safety, all because he was sulking and unprepared to check it out. He had trained as a mechanic when he was younger and he knew more than enough to check that it would be safe and roadworthy.

Ok I will just leave it where it is
and then you can use other til
they come for it

How much is other one a month?

318

How long for?

Was 3 years

How long left?

29 months

This was why we initially agreed to wait and see what I got so we could clear off all the debt and see what was left.

What, your settlement?

Yes we spoke about it

Are you still ok with that?

Not if I have to move out early the
deal was I could stay until I got it

and depending on how much we would clear everything off and I would give you some and I had enough to find a place but it doesn't look like that's going to happen now

True, but nowhere in our agreement did it say you could be abusive and constantly accuse me of stuff. I have no issue with you being here at weekends in the short term provided you stop attacking me.

And that's why I took out the insurance just in case something happened to me before then as if it did nobody gets anything What is short term week 2 weeks a month and as I said I may not be able to stay away all the time

Well if lockdown doesn't end until potentially end of May you won't be able to find somewhere as agencies are closed.

I will stay out of your way as much as possible you just tell me what you want

Ok. I want you to stop sending me nasty texts, to stop accusing me of stuff, to stop dragging children in to ask them inappropriate questions, to not be nasty to me in front of them

and make comments like
'she needs to learn what
you're like' etc etc.

He made a comment in front of Abbi once, he had been accusing me of more things, and announced that 'She should know what you're like..."

If you agree to it regarding the insurance you can pay the mortgage off and the rest goes to Abbi and Jack and if you sell the house then they get my share less the money your Mum and Dad gave us for deposit and also the 5k your Dad gave I think between them it was 23k

That is blackmail

No it's not you are still getting money what do you want then

You agreeing to stop harassing me provided I agree to your financial terms is absolute blackmail

It's not I'm putting forward what I would like to happen

I asked you to stop harassing me and your next text was 'if you agree to...'

Ok then you tell me
what you want

I want you to stop harassing me
If you wish to discuss the
insurance then that is a
separate matter and cannot
be linked to whether you
stop harassing me or not.

Ok I won't text you again you can
text me when you want to
discuss anything

Ok, fair enough

5th

Sorry just to let me know I will
probably be back Thursday night
as it's Easter weekend

9th

I might not be back until
Saturday I will see how
tomorrow goes may be
Friday night

Ok thank you for the update

Sorry it's a bit late in
telling you

No problem, Abbi did tell
me that might happen

I was just letting her know
because she is missing me. I may
have an apartment from the end
of next week so I may be able to
stay longer

Ok, that's fine and hopefully
might feel more settled and
eat better

I will be back later today and
leaving on Sunday afternoon

Ok

Are you staying upstairs now

I was pretty much living in my room by this point.

11th

I'm going to take your car to the
car wash is that ok

Yes, thanks

I'm popping out with Abbi do
you want to come

Thanks, but no thanks

Didn't think so
Do you want a bbq for dinner

That's fine, thanks

I might make some punch will you
want some

I'm happy to have some if that's
ok, thanks

What time do you want to eat
Just to let you know I'm going
to go in the morning before
everyone gets up I will tell Abbi

Ok

Sorry I have to do it I would go
tonight if I could I am annoyed
with myself on how I feel about
you but I need to leave

I thought you didn't love me or
fancy me, so I'm not sure what
you mean. But if you have to
go then fair enough

I wasn't asking him if he loved me, or fancied me, I was saying that this is what he had said, so I was confused as to why he was suggesting he had feelings for me.

I wish I didn't
I need to find a way to not see you
I'm sorry but my mind keeps on
playing games with me one
minute I don't want to know you
then the next I miss and love
you I'm confused and I don't

know what to do
Just tell me to stay away and you
don't want any more to do with me

You want me to tell you that?

I can't come back here anymore
Good bye

1

2th

'I'm not drinking that much again '

I think the longest he ever went without a drink, at least for the past ten or so years, was about two days.

With him being away and us no longer together, I was relieved that there were times when he didn't message for days, or if he did they were only to moan, so I didn't respond.

17th

Are you back here this weekend?

Yes did Abbi not tell you

Ok, was just double checking

I will stay away next week and
maybe they can come up for
the weekend

Have you got the apartment
sorted now then?

Yes until the end of the month

at least just got keys

Are you staying the
whole weekend?

Will probably leave on
Sunday why?

Just wondering, especially as
you now have an apartment.

Do you not want me to
come back

I know you are coming back to
see kids.

Yes and i only got keys today I
didn't think I was getting them
til Monday if you don't want
me to come and see them
tell me

I'm not going to stop you seeing
them, you know that.
But if you are going to have them
next week, you might want to
get settled?

So why all the questions about
how long I'm staying and I
still don't know what is
happening at the end of the
moth I still might be going to
either Cambridge or Bury

Not unreasonable for me to ask

is it?
So does that mean you plan
on moving back
permanently then?

Will have to unless I can find
something cheap we have spoken
about it

I know, but last week it seemed
likely that this 2 months working
away would be for longer and
that you could stay as you had
an apartment.

Can we talk about it when I
get back

He changed the goal posts so much, he was going to do this, then that, then it fell through, then it couldn't happen for some reason, or he didn't want to do it, or any other number of things.

Ok but I would like a
calm and stress free
weekend please

18th

Is everything ok
I take it I'm in the wrong again

I was distracted, I've had a shock,
worried about my Dad, sorry if
I wasn't paying attention for
a second and didn't leap at
replying to you

We are popping to the shop do

you want anything

No thanks

20th

How is your Dad have you heard
what happened yet

There was nothing to update him on, which I told him later.

21st

Have you heard anything

He seems fine thanks and
no, nothing else yet

23rd

Just to let you know I might be
back tomorrow as one of the
guys has been diagnosed with
vivid 19 and they saying
everyone getting sent home

That puts us at risk surely?
How long for??

Will be two weeks I will know more
in the morning have just come out
meeting over

Another 2 weeks!

Covid was still very new, no one knew much about what was going on, isolation or anything else and the thought of him being back for at least 2 weeks was too much.

Yes sorry do you want me to try
and find somewhere to go

Like where?

I don't know but if you don't
want me there I will have to try
and find somewhere
I'm only trying to let you know
what's happening

Can't you stay there as you have
the apartment, I'm sure they'll s
till have to pay for the rental?

As I said I will know
more tomorrow

Ok, well let me know as
soon as you know please

If you don't want me there
I will stay in the car all I know
just now is that they want to
send everyone home

He didn't stay in the car, it was just another way to try and make me feel guilty.

24th

I will be back later

For 2 weeks?

Yes can phone you in a bit

I am not happy

Do you think I am

I don't understand why you
can't stay there as they've
paid for apartment

Can I call you to explain
what's happening

He claimed that no one was being allowed to stay, that the company were getting a refund for the rent they had paid out and therefore everyone had to go home.

Abbi used to use his iPad, the same one he had Facebook on and she picked it up to show me something. His account was still open, there was a message that suggested it wasn't a case of him having to come back for 2 weeks, more that he had lost his job and didn't have one to go back to.

After I saw it, I did ask him about it. He said that it was just about him not going back for two weeks.

Did I feel bad that I had looked? Not really, after all, I hadn't gone snooping to find it, it was open on a page on a device his daughter often used.

Ok
Can't you see if you can go to
your sisters?

I will come for weekend and see if
I can sort something out if that's
ok with you

I don't have a choice do I

I will sort something for Monday

He didn't.

28th

He had made a comment to me about him making effort but that I still didn't want him in the house, he then walked out and drove off.

No I don't want you here because
you are unpredictable. You are
nice now but I know how you can
be when you drink and you can
flip in an instant. You had a go
at me at the weekend cos I
didn't say hello

If I'm friends with you, I'll let
my guard down and you could
kick off again. You honestly
don't know the damage those
last few weeks before this
ended caused me. You bullied
me, threatened me, scared
me and Abbi. I can't just wipe
that out.
I still get welfare checks from

Women's Refuge who want to do a risk assessment with me as they know you are back in the house. How the fuck do you think that makes me feel.

As soon as I can I will leave for now I will just stay out your way and ignore you will only communicate via text

And that's your response to my text, says it all

What do you want me to say I'm not a mind reader

After nearly 18 years you clearly don't understand me at all. So nothing, say absolutely nothing.

Can I send something to your printer

Fine

29th

Thank you for saying something

My step-sister had just died unexpectedly and I was worried about my Dad, so I told him I that I was distracted because of this and not really paying much attention to anyone but my Dad.

I understand you are going

through some stuff just now
I'm here for you if you need
some support

30th

I only asked a simple question,
I don't understand why you
got so defensive. I apologised
yesterday and explained that there
was a lot going on for me. Was
simply seeing if everything
was ok with you.

It seems that I hadn't supported him. I really don't know what over, but then again, there often was no real reason why he accused me of things.

Nothing is ok with me I'm
just a piece of shit

I never said that

I will leave when you get
back and you won't here f
rom me again

I'm not asking you to leave.
This is hard on both of us.
I really loved you I don't want you
to be hurting. I can't stop you
going, it is your choice, but I
hope you don't and won't
hurt the kids.

I will never hurt them I
don't even want to hurt you
but I have to go I will just have

to live in the car until things
blow over

I'm really sorry, my client
has arrived so I can't answer t
his now.
I don't want to hurt you either.
Have you decided what you
are doing?

I will speak to you when you
get back

Can we do it by phone so that we
have space?

I'm going to leave but I need
the car

Why do you need the car?

I'm going to sleep in it

You can't do that, if you are
found the police will move
you on. Anyway that could
damage your health.

It's all I can do I told you
once I'm gone I'm gone

There must be another solution?

There's not I have nothing to be
here for it best for everyone
If the police say anything I
will tell them I'm homeless and
what can they do from there

You have your children.
And you might get a job you
can start.

He claimed he had some options of work that meant moving away pretty permanently, back to Scotland even, but nothing came of it.

I'm not going to beg you to stay,
but I'm making it clear that I am
not, in any way forcing you out
of the house.

Sorry I have made my mind up and
it's probably best for everyone in
the long run

Well if that's your decision,
then I have to respect that .
I'm sorry it's got to this point.

At least you can file
for abandonment

I don't even know what
that means.

I have abandoned you

All I know is, it's the children
who will suffer and I've tried
my best to protect them
over this.
I know the term,
I mean file what?

Divorce

I'm sorry, but I already have
grounds for that. Was hoping
to do this more amicably.

I hadn't filed for divorce at this stage, but I had sought advice and been told that I had more than enough grounds based on his unreasonable behaviour.

I have tried to protect them
as well

The difference is I guess,
I'm not abandoning them.

Sorry if that sounds harsh,
not trying to lay a guilt trip,
it's simply fact.

True

Ok, then do what you have to do,
but look after yourself.

Is it ok if I come and talk to you

Yes

I promise I won't get angry

Ok, thank you
Downstairs please

I was in my bedroom, yet again trying to avoid him.

Can I talk to you again

Ok

Can I have some of your rum

He had literally never asked before, he always just took.

Yes

May 2021

1st

I only have £100 to pay into your account.

'Paying into your account,' sounds as though he is doing me a favour, by giving me money, he means the account I pay all the bills from. I had to take over the majority of the bills, including the mortgage, as he failed to pay so many times that, as you, know, we nearly lost our house. There was always an expectation that I would pay, regardless of whether he thought I had money or not and irrespective of the fact that he often earnt more than me.

2nd

I'm popping to Tesco
I actually feel bad and sad that I
put you through what I did and
I'm truly sorry for doing that.

He has dashed off to see a female work colleague who had been physically and emotionally abused by her husband and yes I do see the irony!!

Thank you

It is a shame that it's come to
this we where good

True but sadly there is no going
back now.

That's true I just wanted to say

Thank you

3rd

I'm really glad we are getting
on better

Makes things easier

It does and it's nice
Just to let you know it's
been over between us for
70 days today

I haven't been counting

I have I just thought I would let
you know I thin you allowing
me to give you a cuddle yesterday
brought this back a little and I
never went aht long before

without giving you a cuddle

It was a brief hug that I accepted together with a verbal apology after he returned from seeing his work colleague. The really sad thing is, that I actually believed him this time, I believed that he was sorry, after having seen someone else be abused.

Sorry I think I'm feeling a bit
emotional just now think it's
just hit me how bad was to you

That's fair enough.
I missed being hugged,
it just can't be
you unfortunately.

That's fine I know that
I will try not to mention how I
feel again I just felt like I
needed to tell you

It's fine, it's not a problem.

I have to admit I do miss your
company even when we don't
actually talk to each other

Thank you

I don't know what you are
thanking me for I'm the one
that ruined our marriage
and part of your life

Don't do this to yourself it
won't help.
I said thank you because
you said you enjoy
my company

I do and did enjoy your
company as I said I'm just
feeling a bit emotional just
everything I have said and
done to you has hit like a tonne
of bricks and I'm truly sorry
to have put you through all
that crap

Thank you for
acknowledging that.

I will stop now I don't want
you to get annoyed with me
I just wanted to let you know

Ok and again, thank you

I know this will never happen
but I wish I could just come a
hold for a while

I'm sorry
but it's not a good idea.

I know that's why I said it would
never happen and I totally
understand but I can't
help wishing

Just ignore me I'm being stupid

I was slightly worried that you
were going to start getting
funny with me again as I said
I was feeling uncomfortable.

He had asked to come in my room, then asked to sit on my bed, then just sat there staring at me. I asked what he wanted and he said, "*Just to be close to you*". A few seconds later and with him just staring at me, I asked again what he wanted as I was in bed and feeling very uncomfortable with him there. He said, "*Oh don't bother*" and walked out.

Think I should just go back to
having no emotions or
showing any
I don't know what you
mean by funny

Earlier you said it was nice that
we could talk.
I meant commentsile you just sent
me. We are getting on can we just
continue to do that please.

Yes
I am really glad we are getting
on it's just I'm aching inside I
feel worse now than I ever did
with anger
What is commentsile

Whatever I say now will either
come across as heartless or
giving (false) hope. So can I

suggest you go to bed.
It should have said
comments like...

I will leave you alone I'm only
being open and honest with you
and probably for the first time
ever so you can say what ever
you want to say

Only because what ever you say
will not stop me from feeling
the way I do
I honestly don't want to say
anything, just go to sleep.
I'm sure it will seem
better tomorrow.

I have got really bad pain in
my chest

Have you got pain in your
left arm?

A little bit at the top and bit
tingly at the bottom
At least if I don't wake up
tomorrow you'll get
the insurance
I have been getting this for
about the last 5 or 6 weeks
but this bad it normally
passes in about 10 minutes

This is the first time he had mentioned this.

Do you need to call 111?
Unlikely to be a heart attack if

you've had it several times?

Not just now let me see if it eases
not had it several times
only a few in the weeks
but this will be the second
time this week

I sent him a screenshot of the symptoms of a heart attack, he just kept claiming that he couldn't read it. Despite his many previous claims of being ill in order to manipulate me, I still didn't want anything bad to happen to him.

4th

I know you will probably totally
dismiss what I'm going to say
I'm truly sorry that this has
happened between us but me
knowing now exactly what I put
you through I would do
anything I could for us to get
through this and eventually get
a life together

Again, telling me what I was going to do, or at least assuming, rarely was he right. It was quite common for him to tell me *"You're tired", "You have to get up early", "You should do..."*. All things that I could decide for myself, and yet he thought he knew me well enough to decide how I felt, what I thought and what I should do.

Actually, he was a big fan of telling everyone what they should do and yet he never accepted any form of advice, or suggestion himself.

I can understand that but sorry
I can't go back and I can't
expect you to change for
me, it wouldn't work

Ok now that we know where we
stand maybe in the next few
days we can sit down and
see what we can do and
come up with a compromise
on how we are moving forward
I don't think that sounds right somehow

You say you'd do anything,
I say I can't go back, next thing
you tell me you want me to
give you £10,000 to buy you
out. How am I supposed
to react??

As I am self-employed, I had received a grant from the government for my business due to lockdown. I had made the mistake of leaving the letter (in the envelope) on the kitchen table and he had clearly read it.

I'm sorry the more time I spend
with you the more feeling I start
to get for you so you have it
written so that's it then

I'm sorry, I'm prepared to try
and make this work as best
as possible until you can
move out but I'm sorry,
I can't help how you or I feel.

Your the one in control of
everything you've got

all the evidence in written
and with the police so you just do
what you feel best in doing
I'm not being nasty in any way
I being honest with you
It's totally your choice on
what happens
Can you make the choice on
what you want to do so that I
know what's come up

What do you mean,
choice about what??

The choices he gave me were usually to agree with what I want, or I will be nasty and make life difficult for you.

18:55 It's ok you don't have
to I have so everybody loses out

By everybody he meant my children as well and he knew that no matter what, I wouldn't let anything bad happen to them. He just used them as pawns to try and control me, or to try and get me to agree to things so that they didn't suffer.

18:57 I have no idea what you
are talking about but I think
we need to stop communicating
for a while as we seem to be getting nowhere.
I'm sorry you are sad but there
is nothing I can say to make things better for you.
18:57 I'm done now
18:59 I've tried my best
19:02 You can have everything
I don't care now
19:07 Black my because
I take it send y messages

is abuse as it is then get me arrested
19:10 And not replying it a
ll I need to know I hope
you have a wonderful life
19:20 Good bye I really did love you
19:31 I'm not sorry about the
mess you will have to clean it up
19:35 I won't be here tomorrow
19:50 At the end of the day
all I was asking for was a
way out of this and trying
to compromise but you had
to turn it around to what
you thought so again make
me the bad one you go on to me
that if I don't like the answer
you are just as bad I have
tried this last few days to be
open and honest with you tell you
how I'm feeling of a way
we could resolve this apologetic
and been sincere over it all I
was and thinking was

He often claimed he wanted to sort things out, but he was never prepared to change, he just wanted me to.

19:51 Sorry don't know
what happened things moved about
19:54 And sorry to say this
you told me you never wanted
to be like your mum you have
turned into her

I am not sure why he felt the need to bring my Mum into this. She died in 2011 and as far as I am aware had been nothing but nice and supportive towards him.

19:59 You may sorry will get a
few txts with some home
troughs but I don't care
now because I know you
won't care or best still I won't
be there and you will have
to deal with it
20:00 I going to make Abbi the last ever pudding I do for her I
hope that makes you happy
20:07 Gin vodka and wine
makes a good cocktail
20:09 At least you can keep
all these to build your case up
20:11 So this is why im h
appy to text you all night
until the end
20:12 And it's ok I have
deleted everything of my phone
20:13 I give you
are enjoying this
20:13 Sorry hope
20:14 Because to be
honest I am your lisp
20:14 Loss
20:19 And yet again
I'm not being bullying I
'vejust had enough of
everything and now it's time
20:20 I've done or not
done my best whatever I
can't do anymore
20:20 I really hope you are enjoying this

At around this point I emailed my Women's Refuge worker to tell her he was messaging and it did not seem that he was going to stop. I most definitely was not enjoying it.

20:21 No response means you are

The best thing I did was not respond because this then became harassment when I told him to stop and he didn't, had I responded it would have been a different matter.

20:26 I have said good bye t
o Abbi have told her
I love her whether I'm hear or not

The next day Abbi told me he hadn't said anything to her.

20:27 I really hope you are enjoying this
20:30 And to be honest I
not think but know you are
20:33 Come on give me
some sort of response it
will help me even more
if you don't want to then
on your conscience be
it definitely not mine
20:40 Ok you win again
I hate you I mate life
without you so I'm going
to be nasty now a hope
you're cancer comes back
and you have nobody to
look after you I don't
care anymore not about
you or our children they
can survive you have killed me
20:41 As I said everybody losses now
20:43 You get nothing they
get nothing you get the mess
to clean up goodbye
20:47 He sent me a photo of him holding up a craft knife
he had recently ordered
Good bye

With every message me sent, I tensed up that little bit more, my anxiety grew with each passing minute and I just didn't know what he might do next.

Why didn't I leave? Lockdown had dictated where we could go and who we could see and I just felt trapped.

A few days later a parcel arrived containing a tube of anesthetic gel.

My son was there when I opened it and it really upset him. He asked me to put it somewhere out of sight.

I am not sure I slept much. I was listening out for every sound and was worried what I might wake up to.

5th

I heard him moving about in the morning, so I knew he was alive. It sounded like he was packing, but I stayed in my room until I not only heard the door shut, but his car leave.

07:40 You win I've gone

I called 101 and reported what had happened. They said someone would call me back to take a statement but then called to say someone would be coming out instead. It was arranged for 7.30pm because I had to work.

09:38 I'm just a horrible and
nasty person a shit father
and no good for anything
so this probably the best for everybody
12:22 He called
12:23 – "*Can I please try and speak to you. Please.*"
12:29 He called
12:30 – "*Please talk to me. I need help. Badly. I'm so sorry but please help me.*"
12:42 He called

12:43 – "*Please help me, I'm begging you. I really am, I'm begging you. Please help me.*"
12:50 He called
I blocked his number after advice from the police.
12:36 I'm begging for help
13:14 I hope you have a
wonderful life now
13:18 At least I know now
you will never contact me again
13:28 Can stop getting the p
olice calling me I'm just ignoring them now
13:49 I really hope you are happy now
15:01 You do realise that now
everybody is going to loose out
I really do hope the next 18 years
is better than the last
It doesn't hurt when you pour vodka on it
15:46 I have just about got to where I want be

I gave my statement today. As one officer took me through the events the other one read all the messages he had sent. He actually said, "That's disgusting" when he read the one about hoping my cancer came back.

I had to complete another risk assessment form.

6th

He called -
10:05
10:41
13:04
14:21
15:39
15:52
19:23

He kept messaging my children, telling them to tell me he was coming to the house and he didn't care. At one point he said he was on his way, and I panicked, locked down my house and sat there not really knowing what to do.

But time passed and I decided there was no way I was going to live in fear of this man, so I unlocked doors and windows that didn't need to be locked and got on with my day.

Shortly after, he messaged my daughter to say that his Mum said hello (she died when he was 14 or 15). I took her phone away from her because I was very concerned about what he might say to her. I did talk to her about it and explained why, she understood.

I got a call from a police officer today telling me that she had to take a statement. I told her I had done it already, she said it was for something else, but I said I had done it. I told her he had been messaging, she said "*that's not good*" and asked me to send her screenshots and she would look into the statement.

I never heard from her again.

7th

Today he sent my daughter a picture of his Mum's gravestone.

I had a call from another police officer today telling me he had to take my statement and again I told him I had done this.

He told me that he thought he had been arrested in Mersea.

10th

I got another call from the police today to tell me he had

been released. I was worried what would happen but he assured me he would have been warned about things.

I later found out that he had been released on the 9th, more than 24 hours before I was told about it.

11th-15th

After seeking advice from a family member, who is an ex-police officer and being advised that I ought to have been told what bail conditions had been set, I spent the week trying to find out this information.

I called and was promised a return call from the officer, no call.

13th

My Dad called me to tell me he had bumped into him at Tesco. I'm not exaggerating when I tell you I felt instantly sick, partly because this meant that he was likely staying locally (the police had not advised me as to where he was staying).

He tried to persuade Dad to convince me to drop the charges, repeating that he couldn't go to prison.

My dad told me that he looked terrified, and he kept saying he didn't want to go to prison, Dad told him that I didn't want him to go to prison, but the decision wasn't mine.

14th

I was at the supermarket with my son when he started to get texts from him. He was trying to get my son to convince me to drop the charges. My son didn't know what to say and I really didn't want him to get stuck in the middle. I said to just tell him that I couldn't make any decision until I had spoken to the police but I was not pushing for him to go to prison.

He wouldn't stop with the messages so in the end I just told my son to say that he might be breaching his bail conditions and he needed to stop. Eventually he did.

I called the police again, they claimed they couldn't find the officer and put me through to the same department as before, bearing in mind that it was now the 15th, and I finally was told his conditions and promised a call. No one called, but at least I knew he couldn't contact me directly or indirectly, he was also prohibited from attending my address.

The police later accepted it as a "fair comment", that had I been told about his bail conditions and therefore would have known to report him that the later incidents may not have happened.

Chaper 6
Endings

May 15th

My son saw his Dad today, against my better judgement but he wanted to as he had a problem with his scooter.

He wasn't gone long but was very distressed when he came home, yelling that he didn't want to be involved. Honestly I let him because I could understand how he felt and I wasn't going to tell him off.

It later turned out that his Dad kept telling him that he was living in a tent, that he was going to run out of money, that he had nowhere to go and couldn't go to prison.

17th

I posted something on my work social media page and he left a comment.

Shortly after, he texted me this –

I know I have broken my bail by sending you this. All I wanted was some help from you to find somewhere as the more time I spent with you the more I love you I hope you read this and don't go to the police as I will get arrested straight away

I don't want to go to jail over this as I don't think it will help anyone all I want to do is sort things out between us I have left you an envelope in the car I hope you get it. It's got letter for you and the children I can't live like this anymore I'm sorry and I will always love you Tell Jack i'm sorry to get him evolved but he was the only one I could contact

I give up now
I have nothing

I called my son to see if he knew where his Dad might be, as he had only seen him a couple of days ago. He didn't, but I decided, if he really was living in a tent as he had claimed, that there were a limited number of places he could be locally, so I decided to have a quick drive around to look for him.

My son was on his way back from my dad's and I knew my daughter was safe, as my niece was due to arrive shortly.

I had been gone for about 30 minutes when the first call came. I didn't realise it was him, as I had only seen the number once before (when he texted) and I didn't recognise it.

He asked me not to hang up or call the police.

I asked him where he was and if he was alright.

He just kept sobbing down the phone and telling me he had hurt himself.

He hung up.

Two minutes later he called again.

He kept saying he didn't want to go to prison, but wouldn't tell me where he was.

I asked if he was ok. Actually I was quite scared and remember screaming at him to tell me where he was so I could get to him, or I would call the police.

He told me.

He was about two minutes from my house.

I told him I was on my way and called my sister because firstly, he wasn't allowed near me and honestly, I'm not that keen on blood and she is first-aid trained.

He called again a few mins later and I told him I was on my way.

I grabbed my sister and we headed to his location. Just as we were approaching my village, he called again, this time telling me he didn't need my help and was going to leave.

I told him I was almost there and to stay where he was.

When I saw his car, on a rather narrow road, I pulled over and slightly blocked him, and as my sister got out of the car, I shouted, "*What have you done?*" He held his arm up to me and showed me some minimal cuts and a small amount of blood.

He wouldn't let my sister in the car and started to edge towards me. I didn't feel safe, so I got out his way.

As he sped off, I turned around and my niece called to say she was almost at my house. Within seconds she called back to say she had seen him parked up about a quarter of a mile from where I was.

As I found him, I will admit I leapt out the car and screamed at him

"*What the fuck do you think you are doing?*"

He told me, "*You've done this, you've caused this*".

I knew I hadn't but there was just no getting through to him.

He showed me his arm again and I could see that the cuts were minor.

He handed me an envelope and told me he was going to drive into the river.

I told him not to be stupid.

He told me he was going to drive into the house.

I told him not to be stupid, but he sped off.

I remember driving up the very slight hill to my house (which was about 20 or so seconds away) and saying to my sister that I couldn't see his car, but then as I got closer I could see it, half in my kitchen.

I don't fully remember exactly what happened and when at this point.

I could see people everywhere and I remember leaping out of the car and I was later told I screamed something.

I could hear my son on the phone and I knew my sister had called 999. But honestly, it all remains a little fuzzy.

I remember walking into my house to check on my daughter, and told my niece to take her to my dad's house and I think my son was still on the phone.

My daughter was taken away by my niece and sister and my son, when he finally got off the phone to the emergency services, ran, he just ran away from the house. I didn't know until later that when he arrived at my Dad's he collapsed on the stairs incoherent and sobbing. He was so upset that my Dad decided to take him out of the village and to a friend's house. Luckily, I am friends with his parents and they welcomed him in. They didn't know what had happened, but they knew something had.

The police called my friend as they wanted to speak to my son, but she called me to update me.

When I spoke to Jack, his first question was whether I had seen Hamish, our cat. He said that he had better not have hurt Hamish and was only reassured when I managed to find the cat and take a photo to send him.

He also told me that he really didn't want to give a statement, but he would if I needed him to. I wasn't going to put him through that and risk him having to give evidence against his father, so I told the police he couldn't be interviewed.

People were asking me questions about him, someone asked me his date of birth, then someone asked me something else and I remember saying

"*Leave him in the fucking car.*"

I never even attempted to go near him, I don't know why, but then I didn't really know what I was doing at this point, so I guess I will never know.

He was I believe unconscious when people got to him, not badly injured I don't think, well I was later told that he walked to the ambulance and when challenged by my niece that he could have hit her (he missed her by only an inch or two), he told her she should be grateful.

I don't really know what happened for the rest of the day. I remember the police, an ambulance and fire engine. I do remember trying to convince someone to let me into the ambulance, but he just looked at me.

I remember my next door neighbours bought me a chair, another one gave me a brandy (yuk, but very kind of them) and another one hugged me and pretty much gave over her house to me and the police.

Someone else tried to hug me and people kept trying to get me to sit down, but I couldn't stay still. I remember calling a friend in such a panic, that they had to remind me to breathe.

I remember a lot of very nosy people standing around and I recall one officer shaking his head in disbelief when he told me the reason so many people were standing around was due to a rumour about a man running around with a knife, so they all came out to see…

One neighbour who hadn't been there when it happened arrived back and carried on so much, he had to be told to calm down or he would be arrested. This is the same one who told me later, when I was clearly distressed, that it wasn't all about me.

I had friends messaging me to check I was okay, rumours having done the rounds, and a few people I knew turned up to ask if I was alright.

He was arrested of course, initially for dangerous driving and drink driving, but the minute the first detective arrived, he was also arrested for attempted murder. It's mad, but I remember asking him if they would keep an eye on him. I think I was worried he might try and hurt himself, God only knows why, because he wasn't worried about hurting any of us.

I escaped for a few minutes to a friend's house, who sat me down and gave me a drink. I wasn't there long before my sister called to say the police were looking for me, but my friend wouldn't let me leave until I had finished my drink.

I gave statements, and seemed to wander between my street and my Dad's house, feeling rather lost I guess.

Abbi thought it had been an accident, when he drove into the house. She thought his foot had slipped and he had done it by accident. I couldn't bring myself to tell her that it had been deliberate. I even told the police she thought it was an accident because I didn't want them to say anything different in front of her.

But I do remember at one point, standing in the middle of the road, between the fire engine, ambulance and police car, feeling as if I was standing in a disaster movie, feeling ever so small, it was like the world was happening all around me but I was very much alone. I know that sounds a bit bizarre but it was how I felt.

The day gradually passed, Abbi was checked out by a fireman, and she and I had to give first accounts. The police took items from me as evidence, items that they later destroyed without my knowledge or permission and initially attempted to cover up what they had done. My house was inspected and I was told I couldn't go into it. I was allowed back in with the structural engineer to grab some clothes but that was it.

I was eventually allowed to leave, being told I would be fully interviewed the next day and my house was boarded up.

What followed was days of interviews, more risk assessment forms, more referrals to domestic abuse agencies, actually I say that, but the police never sent the referral off.

On the day it happened, the first detective on scene told me that I would have to be interviewed by a specially trained officer as I needed to give my statement by video.

The next day a young officer turned up, not a specially trained one, and he told me that a detective would be taking my statement. Many calls backwards and forwards later, not only did a detective not arrive, but as I wasn't a witness, I couldn't be interviewed by video. The officer completing the statement was clearly quite new, he ran out of battery on his camera and I had to correct the statement in many places.

A day or so later, two detectives arrived for yet more statements, at least that is my recollection and they told me that I was classed as an intimidated victim and as such they could apply for screens to be around me so I couldn't see him. I agreed because they told me whilst I could change my mind on the day, if I didn't ask now, that it couldn't be arranged at short notice.

One of the police officers that I dealt with told me that he had been an accident investigator for many years and that he had driven into the weakest part of the house. He commented that he could have driven into it at 100 miles an hour and not done himself much damage. He would have been aware of this, based on his history as a mechanic and the structure knowledge he had for his various jobs.

I was asked if I wanted them to apply for information about him via Claire's Law. I said yes and they told me it would take about six weeks and they would then tell me if there was anything. As it turns out, the officer later claimed he couldn't remember if he had applied when I had asked (I didn't, they offered), and some seven odd months later, after I chased it several times, I was told that I couldn't be told anything, because as he was in prison, that spoke of his character anyway.

All of this was in between other support agencies contacting me, me fighting insurance companies to try and claim against him. I couldn't, I was told, because he was named on the mortgage and as such he would be deemed to have benefited from any improvement.

20th

I told his family today that he had been arrested. The truth is, I thought someone should know, so I messaged his sister-in-law. His brother called me and said that they had seen him, as he had actually gone to Scotland when he said he had, after he left and before he was arrested, but he hadn't said much, and that he had clammed up when they started asking questions.

They are the only two members of his family that I have spoken to, and they have been very supportive, asking me to stay in touch and always there if I ever want to talk to them.

Over the next week or so, we also had to arrange builders to make the house safe and start on repairs, luckily Dad stepped in and found a builder he had used before and sorted it all out with him.

He had caused over £18,000 worth of damage to my house, not including the food we lost because power had to be turned off, the new crockery, glasses, cups etc. we needed, or the extra clothes and toiletries I had to buy for my children. Now it might seem strange to you, but I also replaced all bedding and towels because none of us could bare to use anything he had touched.

I still find glass now and then, I honestly don't think I will ever fully get rid of it all.

I couldn't claim against my white goods insurance, because it was deliberate and not accidental.

Sky won't let me change anything because it is in his name, so, I am still paying for his phone because they told me that if I stopped paying, they would come after me for the money as it had been coming out of my account. I did later send him a pre-typed letter to send to Sky asking them to change the account into my name, but either he didn't send it, or Sky ignored it, because it is still in his name at present.

I have had to fight for everything. I have had to research information, make various applications, and do everything myself.

And every time I have to go through this, I have to explain everything all over again, I just can't escape from it, because it is constantly brought back to me.

I was told the date of his initial court hearing and that although the police thought he would be kept on remand they didn't know. I checked the court listing and found the time of the hearing. As time ticked past, I got more anxious but I still didn't hear anything, so I called the officer who had been in charge of the case, he didn't even know it was over but said he would find out for me.

He pleaded guilty, but they didn't know if he was being kept on remand or not, so I had to wait. I had dropped my daughter at school today, delivered her right into the school office, even though she would normally have walked, because I did not know if she would be safe if he was out.

Her school had been really good to be honest. They called the day after it happened, someone having clearly heard what had gone on, and they offered for Abbi to go back to school as they felt they could help support her. Sad to say that my son's school were not supportive in the slightest.

He was being remanded and I stood in my friend's garden and cried because I was so relieved.

I was told that sentencing was taking place in Cambridge on the 26th June, but told that dates can change.

A week or so later Abbi said to me, "*Mummy, I was in the house.*" God I could have cried, and I hugged her so tight. "*I know sweetheart*" was all I could manage, because even then, she hadn't fully comprehended what could have happened, if she had walked into the kitchen at that moment in time. Even now I can't even bring myself to go there and if I didn't already hate him, that fact that he recklessly put the life of his daughter in potential danger, just to hurt me, would be the thing that pushed me to that place.

The day we first decided that we had to go back into the house to start clearing the kitchen before the builders arrived, I was very distressed. I struggle to breath sometimes and the dust was really bad. We had no help because the rules around Covid prevented anyone else coming, so it was just me, Jack and Abbi. It really broke my heart when after seeing me struggling to breath and actually to cope, Abbi hugged me and said "*We shouldn't have to go through this.*" She was right, we shouldn't and yet, we literally had no choice but to get on with it, so we did.

June 2020

It got to the 25th and I had heard nothing, so I had to contact Victims Hub to find out what was going on. Eventually, after very little help from them, I found out it was taking place, at 10am, not at Cambridge as I had been told, but at Peterborough Crown Court.

I told no one, except one friend, someone I totally trusted but who I knew couldn't come with me even if I wanted them to. I understand that you might be wondering why I did this, why I didn't tell anyone else, or take someone as support. The answer is quite simple really, I knew I had to read out my victim statement, and in it were things nobody knew, and I didn't want them to know. I was already feeling as if my life had become public knowledge, but this, this I was doing on my own.

I got to the court, after having got lost, but I made it. It was a complete shambles, with no one having much of a clue what they were doing. It was all blamed on Covid. "It's my first day back in court, so I don't know what they are doing", said the woman there to offer support. It honestly would have been better if she wasn't there, as she was full of patronising platitudes.

I remember pacing up and down because I was so anxious at having to see him, I felt sick and yet she rambled on and on. Helpful comments like "*Well at least after this you can move on*", "*I can't even make you a cup of tea*", she rambled on about Covid and all the things they couldn't do, to the point that I actually said "*But you still have phones right?*"

You know what, I can't even remember it all but I do remember thinking, as she rambled on and on that I was so glad I wasn't a rape victim having to put up with this. She had no clue. I was quiet because I was anxious and yet she just felt the need to fill the empty air, I just wanted her to be quiet, no, that's not quite accurate, I actually wanted her to just shut the hell up!

She had no idea which court we were in, or if he would even be there, so off she went again to try and find out.

I sound very ungrateful I know, but with the confusion around the court venue, getting lost trying to find it and with anxiety raging at the thought of having to face this man, I wasn't feeling my normal, calm and positive self.

I appreciate that Covid affected so many things and that everything was new, but when the support you are told you will get was not there and the person meant to help you seemed to have no clue about how a witness, an intimated one at that, might be feeling, I am afraid I didn't have the mental space to cope with all of this.

Someone from the Prosecutor's office arrived to tell me he would be appearing by video link and wouldn't actually be there. Now you might think I would have been relieved at this, but I had put myself in this horrid position so that I could face him, only now I couldn't.

They told me they knew this was a problem, that victims weren't being told this, as it had been mentioned in a meeting, but was of absolutely no help to me, because it hadn't stopped me being put in the same position, not knowing that he wouldn't be at the hearing in person so to speak. Had I known he wouldn't be there, I may very well not have gone.

Finally we got into court and I could see him on the screen and although it might sound mad, I went from shaking and feeling sick, to a ridiculous urge to wave at him and laugh. He couldn't see me at this point, so I was told. He would only see me when I gave my statement.

It did drag on a bit, I know he lied, although it was his Defence Solicitor who spoke on his behalf. After pointing out to the Prosecutor that she had his date of birth wrong, I discovered that not only had he used aliases in the past, but that he had three convictions. I didn't discover what for until a few days later, but I guess I shouldn't have been surprised that they were for theft.

I had to read out my victim impact statement. I tried so hard to keep it together, but in the silence of the court I just couldn't stop tears from coming and I hated that he saw me so distressed. But I got through it and finally sat down again.

And do you know what the Judge, who had already seen this said? He said it was broad reaching and he had to be mindful he was only dealing with the current offences.

Now I get where he was coming from, but everyone had seen my statement. Why didn't someone tell me I only had to write about that time period? I had specifically asked the police how far to go back and wrote it based on their advice.

The Judge, in his summing up, praised my compassion, because I had attempted to find and help him, rather than simply calling the police. He also made it very clear that he believed all of his actions were an attempt to cause me maximum distress.

And after all that, he gave him forty months, for the crimes of criminal damage (recklessly endangering life), dangerous driving and stalking (with fear of violence).

Of which he would only serve twenty months. I did manage to get an indefinite restraining order, which stated that he could not attend my address, or contact me directly or indirectly except about the children and through a 3rd party extended to cover the whole of the village I live in, as my daughter goes to school there.

I left there before it was quite finished because I was so distressed that he had gotten such a short sentence (based on what had been suggested to me) and also, I was rather afraid I might say something.

I left the courtroom and went to the toilet, as I came out I heard the Prosecutor call me, I turned round and shouted *"You might as well have just slapped him on the wrists and told him not to do it again."* I was absolutely beside myself at the injustice of it.

How I made it back to my car I don't know, but I called the one person who knew I was going to court. I couldn't even bring myself to look at them, I was that distraught and angry. Luckily they stayed very calm and pointed out that when I calmed down I would realise that I had got what I wanted, I was away from him.

My plan had been to tell my children and Dad and then tell everyone else what had happened. But the police never gave me the chance, because before my children had come home from school, a friend sent me a screenshot from the Cambridgeshire Police Facebook page, clearly showing what had happened.

Everyone knew before my children and I was genuinely distraught. Since making a complaint, I have been told that the issue of not contacting victims of domestic abuse before court case details were posted on social media would be looked at. The officer I spoke to said he completely agreed and felt that although the police were legally allowed to report this, after all, it was a win for them, morally he did agree that we victims should at least be warned it was going to happen.

Three days later I was told the case was going back to court as there was an issue, and yet no one at Victim's Hub knew why. It took three different conversations to find out that it was something to do with sentencing. I told my dad in panic that I was worried they were going to reduce it, again, I don't think I slept much that night.

So, back to court I went. I sat there on my own for well over an hour due to technical difficulties before the Prosecutor came and spoke to me. It was she who had contacted the Judge to question the decision as she had realised the figures did not add up. She was ready to appeal, she told me, when the Judge realised that he had made a mathematical error (his words). He meant to give him forty eight months, meaning just another four months in prison, but I hoped that that was at least the end of it.

July 2020

I found out that when Dad was in Australia with my nephew, some months after my Mum had died, he had stolen a cheque and cashed it for £300.

August 2020

We could finally properly move back home.

I came home and my son handed me two pieces of folded up paper. Their father had sent birthday notes to them. I stood there shaking as I read them, and why they arrived in August, a whole month early I have no idea, but my son was not in the slightest bit interested, especially as his said, '*I hope you get the car you want*'. My son, bless him, said, '*Mum, how the fuck does he think I'm going to be able to do that after what he's done?*'. I could hardly be cross, because he was right.

We decided not to give Abbi hers as there was no way I wanted her to be upset on her birthday, although I did plan to keep it so she could have it when she was older (she has since been told about it and seen it and understands why I kept it from her initially).

I tried to head off a debt collector once, because I didn't want my son to have to deal with it, but he wouldn't hand me the letter, he had to post it through the door. Once I had explained to him what had happened, he was very understanding and promised to update his office so that I would be left alone. But I had to go through it again.

I have window alarms now, fitted by the police.

My phone number is registered with them, so if I call 999, they will know.

September 2020

Another letter arrived today –

Dear Jack and Abbi

I hope you Both had a GREAT and Wonderful Birthday.

Im Sorry that I Wasn't there for you Both But I was thinking about you Both.

I hope you Both Got what you WANTED

I Want to try and Keep in Touch With you Both As much as I CAN.

I Do Wish that I could have Sorted things out With Mum But I think she hATES Me THAT Much that is not Going to happen.

So this is Just a Quick not to let you Know That I will miss and Love you All forever.

So look After yourself and Look after Abbi

X

P.S.

I am Truly Sorry for EVERYTHING That has happened and I hope that you can forgive ME.

Will I ever get used to this? Am I always going to shake when a letter arrives?

October 2020

I got a call from the Victim Liaison at the Probation Service today. It seems that the Probation Officer based in the prison realised he had been sending letters and wanted to check whose address it was. Once they determined it was mine, I was told that this was a breach of his Restraining Order (RO).

And then it got ridiculous…

The prison claimed they didn't have a copy of the RO.

They said that the letters had slipped through, because although they had my name, no one had thought to associate a letter address to my home address and with my surname on it, with me.

They then claimed I couldn't complain to them because I wasn't allowed to be told where he was due to Data Protection but gave out an email address I could contact.

The more senior management at the Probation Service said, no, I had to complain to the prison.

The prison said no.

I did at this stage point out the ridiculousness of this, as the prison name, wing and even cell number were written on the letters he had sent!

This saga continued as the prison took so long to reply to anything, citing shifts patterns as the issue.

Honestly, I just wanted him to stop (no one could tell me if he had been told to stop) and for him to know that I had not reported this, that the Probation Officer had, because I didn't want him spending the next eighteen months thinking I'd stopped him from contacting his children.

Calls and emails continued sporadically, but nothing was resolved.

November 2020

Something major happened today, well it might seem trivial you, I was going to bed, I was about to pick up my purse off the kitchen table and take it with me, but I didn't, I left it there and I didn't worry. And you know what, it was still there, with the same amount of money, the next morning.

December 2020

I've been diagnosed with PTSD. I often shake, feel faint for no apparent reason, can tremble constantly for days at a time and get breathless easily. My son often shops with me and it's not unusual for me to be gripping the trolley really tightly as I try to control my breathing. The anxiety sometimes kicks in and I've even thought I've seen him.

I was at home one morning getting ready and as I went to walk into my bedroom I smelt him. It was so strong that I gasped, stepped backwards and looked down the stairs, honestly expecting to see him.

But those things aside, the dreams have been the worst. I'm stuck in them and I can't escape. They vary in theme but it is like he haunts me sometimes, even to the point where I wake with relief from a dream, only to fall asleep and end up in another one. I've had to develop coping mechanisms to feel safe falling asleep.

February 2021

I received a call from a Suffolk Police Officer who asked me if I had heard of anything happening? That was it, I kid you not. So I asked if this was about him and he said yes.

It seems that the prison had reported a breach of RO as he had tried to write to my address again in January 2021. I guess now I knew they hadn't told him to stop.

They knew nothing about the first two, so I had to explain everything.

They insisted they took it seriously and it would be investigated and someone from my local area would come out and speak to me.

No one came, but I did get a call from another Suffolk officer and had to go through it all again. She was clearly new to the job and struggled, it seemed to get anything from the prison (it was later confirmed to me that she was very new to the job).

Again it continued, statements, phone calls, risk assessments, delays, emails and on and on, it was exhausting.

March 2021

Eventually I was told he would be interviewed provided a solicitor was available. When I was updated, I will admit that I laughed, because it seems he claimed that as the prison check his mail and they sent it to me, that he thought they were the 3rd party. There is no way this man, who I had known for more than seventeen years had come up with that on his own.

Anyway, I was told it was going to the CPS.

I was feeling so very frustrated at this point, one agnecy telling me one thing, another one telling me something else. No one could tell me the truth of anything it seemed, because they didn't know.

Every day without him was a step towards feeling better about me and life in general, and yet, he would pop up now and then, cause a problem and I would be dragged back into his madness.

I just wanted someone to stop him from being able to contact us ever again.

April 2021

As I am still classed as high risk, my case was sent to a special department within the police to be assessed. They decided that as he didn't address them to me, and I wasn't mentioned (except of course I was), that they were taking no further action against him.

I was bloody angry by now. Two different police forces involved, or at least were meant to be, the probation service and the prison all involved in this. I had to repeat my story time and time again, be dragged back into this situation time and time again, all for them to decide that they were not going to do anything at all.

They put me through all this, only to decide they were doing nothing.

The police said the probation shouldn't have given me advice as it was wrong and that only they should have. They said my expectations were not managed well at all, as this is not the outcome I was led to believe would happen.

They have said he can no longer write to my address however, but I will wait and see because I have lost all faith in them.

I finished paying off another one of his debts this month.

Whilst writing this book, I found an email on an old laptop that I sent to him on 25th August 2015 –

If you can't hold your promise not to get pissed off, then DO NOT READ THIS.

You moan about work all the time and it gets to me sometimes. No one knows what they are doing according to you, and you are always right, that is what it is like at home sometimes too. You don't understand the fear that goes through me when you threaten to quit.

You treat me like an ATM and then get nasty/aggressive when I dare to mention you repaying it and yet if I borrow a fiver from you, you ask almost instantly when I will be repaying it.

I know it pisses you off but money does worry me, we were in such a bad place a several years ago, that I genuinely do not think I could go through that again, so it angers/disappoints me when you put it at risk because you can't manage your money. I honestly thought our life together is more important than you smoking and drinking (and yes I don't think I shall ever get over that other child, whose payments have driven us over the edge in the past).

Jack and I have a warning system in place to let each other know when you are in a bad mood, as we know that when you are one or both of us will suffer.

You have embarrassed me in public - shouting, swearing, sleeping in the car, abandoning me (at my sisters - and when I and you thought I was pregnant), smashing in 2 front doors, threatening people and who was left to sort it out - me!

You tell me you don't like things I do/or that I have done stuff but when I ask you for specifics so I can stop/change or tell you tough, you always say 'I don't know'. You get the hump with us because we don't do what you want/behave how you want and yet you never tell us what you expect, so we can never get it right.

You bully me and Jack sometimes - e.g. you say shall I cook you something (no), are you sure, I will (no thanks), I don't mind (no), right I'm going to cook you something. You don't listen to me. You frequently threatening to hit/punch Jack.

You never compliment me (unless I point it out) or tell me anything positive. You have told me once since we have been together that you are proud of me, and you were drunk.

I have supported you, lied for you (about why he hadn't gone with me to something we had been invited), defended you, looked for jobs for you, written and re-written your cv for you, spoken to agencies and arranged interviews for you and yet it never seems enough.

I am a reasonably happy person most of the time, but on the odd occasion when I am not, you are really nasty to me.

Maybe I am just fed up of putting up with this for years and years, maybe I want a husband who loves me no matter what, rather than one who seems to love me only when he is in a good mood and only if I behave myself.

Why have I not told you this before? Well I have tried to tell you some of it, but you have either gone sullen or got nasty and over the years I have given up. It is probably why I get ill sometimes, because I am not allowed to get it off my chest.

I am extremely sad at the moment, wondering whether I can deal with all this crap for another 30 odd years.

I want my lovely husband, the one who can make me laugh, who holds my hand, who loves me, not the one I am sometimes scared of, who spends money he doesn't have and threatens our future, the one who can be a bully.

You still seem to carry old crap with you, what people have done to you in the past and almost lump me in with them. Well if I haven't proved myself to you yet, then I guess I never will.

I'm not perfect, I know that, I can be a pain. However, I do tell you I love (and not just by text), I do support you, I do say sorry (and mean it), I am not violent, or generally aggressive and I don't put our future at risk.

I didn't leave then, because early the following year I was diagnosed with Anaplastic Large Cell Lymphoma.

Chapter 7
Conclusions

May 2021
17th

Today is the anniversary of what he did and this is what I posted -

I didn't know whether to post this or not, but I said I would keep speaking up in the hope that it helps others, so here goes.

A year ago today my ex drove his car into my house, he caused extensive damage and made the house unlivable for several months. He did this whilst on bail for harassment and malicious communication.

I couldn't claim on his car insurance because they said he would benefit. I couldn't claim on my white goods insurance because it was deliberate. He was sentenced to 48 months for criminal damage (recklessly endangering life), dangerous driving and stalking (with fear of violence), and as he will serve just 24 months, he will be out in less than a year.

Not a single month has gone by without more grief or hassle. He has broken his restraining order 3 times and the prison claim they can't monitor all men.

There have been more police investigations, across 2 counties, involving the probation service and the prison.

As it stands, I can't divorce him because I cannot find a solicitor with the capacity to take on a legal aid divorce, they are all too busy. Given that you can only get legal aid for domestic abuse cases, this shows you the extent of the problem.

I am surprised how much it has affected me today, I'm actually shaking writing this. I'm not looking for sympathy, and I certainly don't want to hear comments about how strong I am, onwards and upwards or moving on.

You cannot just move on, a prison sentence for him doesn't allow me to just move on. I have alarms on my windows now, my phone number is registered with the police so if I call, they act quicker, I 'see' him in the supermarket, I regularly have dreams with him in them and although I cope really well, I still sometimes shake for no apparent reason.

Getting away from an abusive relationship isn't the end, in a way it's just the beginning and I now totally understand why some people don't want to go through this legal process. There simply isn't enough understanding and support out there.

If you are in an abusive relationship, please tell someone and stay safe x

For a while I struggled to make sense of it all. It was as if I couldn't connect the man I married, or at least the one I thought I had married, with the man who did this. I remember calling my cousin's husband, a retired long-serving police officer a few days after I'd given yet another statement, and saying to him, "*Is it really that bad? I just can't quite comprehend it.*" "*Karen, he drove into your house*" was his reply.

It all seemed so pointless. It never had to happen, he could have just moved out and stayed a part of his children's lives, been included in family stuff for their benefit, had the opportunity to find a new relationship and start a new chapter in his life. I don't understand why he instead decided to take the action he did and not only land himself in prison, but become an absent father as well. It truly makes no sense to me.

Looking back, I think one of the main turning points was when I spent that month in Spain. It was so lovely to live in a house where the atmosphere was light and bright. There were no arguments, no money was stolen and we didn't have to walk on eggshells. I actually felt free, no one was telling me what to do, what I thought or how I felt. It was heavenly. And I think after that, there really was no going back. I didn't realise it at the time, but things were never going to work out between us after that holiday. I think it was the culmination of this experience of freedom and how I had changed after chemo but I had changed and I was not changing back.

For a long time I used to get angry at myself because I wasn't over it, I used to get frustrated that it still affected me, and more than once I have been at the place of wondering if it was really that bad.

It's funny that, the fact that I question if it was really 'that', as if bad wasn't bad enough. I hear stories from people who have been beaten or raped by their partner, those who have lost babies because they have been punched, kicked or pushed down the stairs and I think that what I went through seems nothing compared to that. And it's true, it's not the same, and I guess I count myself as lucky, but what he did, what he put me and my children through was still abuse. So, whether it was to a greater or lesser degree than what someone else has gone through, the bottom line is still the same, what he did was wrong. Yet I still need to be reminded from time to time, not to dismiss his actions.

A few months after he was sentenced, I mentioned to my son that maybe I should go and see him, not because I want to, but because it might help me to see him as he is now. Before I had quite finished my sentence he said, "*No. Mum you don't want him to see that can still upset you.*" And he was right, when I mentioned this, he would still have upset me, but not now.

I used to get panicky when I was in our local supermarket. No idea why, I don't have any particular memories connected with it and him. And on occasions I have thought that I had seen him, the masks made this worse, as I could never be sure it wasn't him.

I've questioned why I didn't see it. Why did I let it go on for so long? How this man, who isn't the most intelligent man on the planet, managed to control and manipulate me. Did he know he was doing it, or was it just how he behaved?

People tell you that when you are in it you can't see it, that you normalise the behaviour and find ways to deal with it, and that is true. But it still stung beyond belief that I was put through this by a man I used to love, and I did love him, but did he ever really love me, at all? I guess I will never know the answer to this question and I'm not sure it would make any difference if I asked him, he would probably just lie anyway.

Sometimes I felt like giving up, keeping quiet and just fading into the background, but then various people point out that it isn't just about me, it's about all those people who can't speak up. Sometimes I feel the weight of this responsibility on my shoulders, but I know it to be true. I know I'm not some kind of avenging angel who can swoop down and make everything alright. If only I had that power, but I can do what I can, and I will continue to do that for as long as I can.

For many months, probably until after the first anniversary passed, I felt exhausted. I was tired of him, of fighting for justice, having to deal with everything that had come my way because of his actions and the worst thing was, I knew it wouldn't be over any time soon.

I never really had any time off, quite frankly because I couldn't afford it, and although the lockdowns made it harder to see clients in person, I kept working with them when I could. I guess my experiences had simply added another perspective and a greater understanding of another subject that I could use to help my clients.

I became aware of how little people understood what domestic abuse is, how it can start and what it is like to live through it. There are lots of agencies out there, all designed to help, but my clients and other people I know who have been through similar experiences all tell me that talking to those who really do know what they are talking about, rather than theoretical experiences, are the only ones who really understand.

There still seems to be this perception that people who stay in abusive relationships are weak, or maybe even stupid, but that really isn't' the case. The pressure people are put under when they try to leave, or even if they do get out is incredible.

And it changes you. You kind of forget how to feel certain things, you learn to lock emotions away, to keep your opinions to yourself and your whole view of life can become skewed.

I told my counsellor one day that I didn't think I could actually love anyone, not just a partner, but anyone. I asked her what love is. She looked at me and asked if I was asking for a clear cut definition and I said yes. She smiled at me and said "Karen that doesn't exist, it's a feeling, not a definitive description." "But I need to know", I said, "Because I don't get it."

I am sure I must have understood it, I am sure I must have felt love before, but it's been so very long since I have felt it, I mean I know my children love me, my Dad, other family members and my friends, but I honestly don't know what to feel. It's like the wall I started to build around myself got so big that it's become like reinforced steel and if I'm honest, I was scared to break it down.

I am not even sure if I am explaining myself clearly, because it is a strange thing to try and express to others, but he killed something in me and it's been suggested that I've got too strong to love. I don't think that's the case, at least I hope not, because a lot of my strength has come from having no choice but to be, it has come from going through many traumas, it has come from pain, but not all of it, some of it is me, some of it must be inbuilt, and come from a place deep within me. So I guess I am strong, although I hate it when I constantly get told this, because sometimes I don't want to be, sometimes I just want someone to hug me and tell me that it will all be alright and that they are there for me. But would I trust them, would I trust that? I don't know, because not only do I feel that I have lost the ability to love, but I often struggle to trust people as well.

There is little, real, long term help or support and the idea of maybe having to hide yourself away for the rest of your life, just to keep yourself and your children safe is horrifying.

I know I have said this before, but getting out of an abusive relationship really isn't the end of it, it is just the beginning of a really hard slog to get your life back. I'm not saying it isn't worth it, it is, but it takes an incredible level of inner strength to just keep going every single day.

Thinking about it, maybe this helps to explain why a conviction is never really the end, because he may get out in 2022, but I don't know how many years it might take me to fully recover.

Is there an answer?

I see all these initiatives happening now, 'Ask for Ani', the one where we were told that supermarket staff were being trained to help, we've seen the hand signal video and the posts about 'Ask me about buying mascara', all designed to help but honestly they just make me mad, because what happens after this?

We pull women out of abusive situations, but then what? It is such a hard slog, I can fully understand why people don't want to put themselves through it, why they might decide it is just easier to stay. I've even been at this stage recently, wondering if it wouldn't just have been easier to put up with it, than to go through all this, that is how hard it has been. I wouldn't have been, I know that, but I have wondered.

I cannot tell you the stories people have told me since all this happened, tales of beatings ignored by the police, those pulled from their homes and then left with nowhere to go, financial loss, those let down by the system, people terrified that they were going to die at the hands of their abuser. I've been told of false accusations of being a bad mother, being left with nothing, children or grandchilren being withheld, Mum's desperately trying to save their children from abusive fathers and being dismissed and not believed. I've been told about women murdered by their partners and stories of rape, physical, emotional and financial abuse.

Quite frankly, I've been absolutely horrified by the things I have heard, but you know one of the main reasons some of these women talked to me? It's because so few others really understand.

Why don't they just leave? I've heard people comment. Because it isn't that easy is the reply.

At least he didn't hit you. Yes, that is what someone actually said to me. How bad must things in this world be, if not being hit is seen as a good option.

Why do they go back, or take him back? Because it is so bloody hard, I really had no idea of what I was going to have to go through after he finally left.

When I talked to friends whilst all this was happening, out of six of us who had experienced abuse in some form or another, I was the only one to get to court. The ONLY one! How is that right?

Then we have some really common issues:-

Not enough evidence to go to court.

The victims is too traumatised or scared to go to court.

The court gives out community service as a punishment.

If you get a conviction, it never really seems long enough. The Judge at his hearing commented that he was 'mindful' of Covid when handing down his sentence. He may actually have got less time because of Covid.

And even if you do escape, even if you get them sent to prison, what comes next is exhausting and traumatising, so few people seem to understand what you have to cope with after it's 'over'. Everything changes and whilst they will be let out at some point, will you ever be the same again?

I had regular phone meetings with a woman from the JobCentre. It started because I was trying to claim something that it turned out I wasn't allowed to and I told them how frustrated I was. She called me to see if I was ok and put me on her list to call monthly, to see how I was doing. I told her a lot of what I had been through and was still going through. She thanked me more than once for being so open and honest, she told me that she had no idea how hard it was for people in my situation, but knowing my story would help her help others like me.

Where is the education to stop this in the first place? Do you know what domestic abuse is? Did you know that threatening to kill yourself in order to control someone is now against the law? Or that continuing to send messages when someone has told you to stop is harassment? That if you put up with something for six months, you are essentially giving permission to allow it to continue?

I would love to see more support in place for victims (God, I really do hate that word), not just going through this process, but afterwards.

It would be so great if an organisation created something to help people know what they can do in terms of debts, changing the names on bills, benefits, mortgages etc. etc. but centrally, because based on my experience each organisation knows things, but it's never consistent and it's never complete.

I have been advised by one organisation, only to be advised something completely different by another, and even two different people within the same organisation. It is so confusing, especially when you are already trying to cope with the trauma.

Divorce from an abuser needs to be made easier and quicker, why can't judges offer an automatic legal separation on the day of sentencing if the victim wants this? Why is it so very difficult to get help divorcing an abuser?

Why are there so few legal aid solicitors able to take on abuse divorce cases? Why are convicted abusers protected by the Data Protection Act, but not the victims? Why do we have so little say in the matter? Why do people who often have no real experience of these issues, no more knowledge than limited theories, make the laws and decisions on these matters? Why do people have to keep dying, because the law is outdated and often too challenging for people to negotiate? Why aren't sentences more severe? Why is it that you might have to sell your home, in order to pay your abuser in a divorce settlement?

The law needs to be changed so that if someone is convicted of abuse and is never allowed to return to the home, victims can get their partners name taken off bills and not be left paying.

It seems to me, that so much could be done, but it isn't. It's talked about, especially when the subject is flavour of the month, usually after someone has died, or those organisations meant to help and support have been found to have done something very wrong. But then it seems to be forgotten, hidden away almost, at least until the next time something terrible happens.

If I could offer advice to people going through this:-

- Keep a record of what is going on.
- Keep all messages and don't delete them even if you send copies to the police, things can and do go missing.
- If you tell someone to stop messaging and they continue, DO NOT respond, because if you do, it isn't classed as harassment or stalking.
- Please try to tell someone.
- If you are planning to get them out of the house, try to get the bills into your name beforehand, because it is an exhaustive nightmare battling people to get this sorted.
- Don't blame yourself, they are doing this not you.

My life now…

Well now life is so much better and I feel happy pretty much every day.

I am learning to trust and to open myself up to more emotions. I now get to laugh without being told off, which is wonderful. I have friends who are amazing, I have support, and now that people know what I went through, I no longer feel the need to hide it. I mean I don't talk about it all the time, but if something worries me, I am now far more able to speak to friends about it and I even cry now and then.

My social life has started growing again and it is wonderful to be able to go out without being questioned, without someone trying to pick a fight before I leave and to not be accused of doing things I'm not doing. Actually, I think I have gone through more lipstick in 2021 than I probably had for the previous 10 years.

My life has really started to improve over the last few months. I feel his spectre less and less, actually he barely enters my mind, unless it is about getting the divorce sorted. But even then, it's more about me, my children and our future than it is about him.

Someone asked me a while ago if I hated him and I said no. They couldn't understand why I didn't, why I didn't bad mouth him or wish him horrible things. But I explained that I don't actually feel anything about him anymore and that I'm simply not prepared to give him any of my energy, emotion or any space in my head. So as far as I can possibly keep it this way, he simply doesn't exist in my life.

Apart from writing this book, I have started a novel, I have a twice monthly podcast with a friend, where we talk about all things 'life', I have written two more courses and a therapy based book and card set.

My Future?

I plan to build my writing career and use my voice to become a motivational speaker, not just for those who have been through abuse, but to educate more people, those in authority and those who might otherwise become abusers themselves. I want to use my knowledge and experience to help build up women who have been through this, or who may be at risk if they don't find their confidence and self-worth, and I want to move, I just don't know how I will manage it, or where I will go. I want my children to be safe and happy and I want a new life, I think I deserve that if I am honest.

My Children…

The reason I have not included too much about my children is to protect them and because I don't want to put words in their mouths.

But as things stand, my son wants nothing to do with his father ever again, and my daughter, was swinging between occasionally missing him (although this was getting less) and being very protective of me, but recently told me that she doesn't want to see him. She is actually scared of what he might do to her, or that he might hurt her to get to me. She thinks the restraining order will keep me safe and she wants one to stop him going near her as well now. She understood why she couldn't see him, and when she has asked me questions about him, I have answered as honestly as I can. I never bad-mouth him in front of them, I say never, I do slip sometimes, when something has happened, but I never set out to.

Out of all of us, she was the only one who kind of still liked him at the end, the only one he was actually nice to. She told me about a year after it happened, that a week or so before he left, that he told her that she was the only one of us he loved.

Abbi told me once that she wanted to go and see him in prison, when I asked why, she told me that she wanted to ask him why he had done it. "*I'm not sure he knows and you probably won't get the truth anyway*" is what I told her. Sadly her response was something along the lines of yes, he would probably just lie.

When we reached the one year anniversary, Abbi told me that the noise had been so loud when the car hit the house. I felt so bad, because I had never thought to ask her about that particular element, but then she went on to say, "*I'm glad I hadn't gone into the kitchen to get that drink*" and I didn't really know what to say, too much emotion was stuck in my throat. She knew he had originally been arrested for attempted murder, but I don't think she realised that that had essentially been because of her being in the house.

And Jack? Well he is doing really well in his education and has very clear plans as to what he wants to do with his life and he is far less angry now.

He does often have a rather black and white view of the world, and is honest in his thoughts and feelings. He's supported me and given me strength in writing this book.

The journey was hard and I wish that I had made different choices along the way, but I can truthfully say that now I am so much happier so the struggle was worth it.

By the time this book is released, so will he have been.

Emergency Numbers

Police Emergency – 999. If you can't speak and you are calling from a mobile, press 55 when prompted, cough or make a noise and they will know you need help.

Police Non-emergency – 101

National Domestic Abuse Helpline – 0808 2000 247

About the Author

Karen still lives in the family home in Cambridgeshire with her two children and Hamish the cat.